Lester B. Pearson

ALSO IN THE
EXTRAORDINARY CANADIANS
SERIES:

SERIES EDITOR:
John Ralston Saul

Lester B. Pearson

by ANDREW COHEN

With an Introduction by
John Ralston Saul
SERIES EDITOR

EXTRAORDINARY
CANADIANS

PENGUIN CANADA

Published by the Penguin Group

Penguin Group (Canada), 90 Eglinton Avenue East, Suite 700,
Toronto, Ontario, Canada M4P 2Y3 (a division of Pearson Canada Inc.)

Penguin Group (USA) Inc., 375 Hudson Street, New York, New York 10014, U.S.A.
Penguin Books Ltd, 80 Strand, London WC2R 0RL, England
Penguin Ireland, 25 St Stephen's Green, Dublin 2, Ireland
(a division of Penguin Books Ltd)
Penguin Group (Australia), 250 Camberwell Road, Camberwell, Victoria 3124, Australia
(a division of Pearson Australia Group Pty Ltd)
Penguin Books India Pvt Ltd, 11 Community Centre, Panchsheel Park,
New Delhi – 110 017, India
Penguin Group (NZ), 67 Apollo Drive, Rosedale, North Shore 0745, Auckland,
New Zealand (a division of Pearson New Zealand Ltd)
Penguin Books (South Africa) (Pty) Ltd, 24 Sturdee Avenue, Rosebank,
Johannesburg 2196, South Africa

Penguin Books Ltd, Registered Offices: 80 Strand, London WC2R 0RL, England

First published 2008

1 2 3 4 5 6 7 8 9 10 (RRD)

Copyright © Andrew Cohen, 2008
Introduction copyright © John Ralston Saul, 2008

Manufactured in the U.S.A.

LIBRARY AND ARCHIVES CANADA CATALOGUING IN PUBLICATION

Cohen, Andrew, 1955–
Lester B. Pearson / Andrew Cohen.

(Extraordinary Canadians)
Includes bibliographical references.
ISBN 978-0-670-06738-1

1. Pearson, Lester B., 1897–1972. 2. Canada—Politics and
government—1963–1968. 3. Canada—Politics and government—
1957–1963. 4. Canada—Politics and government—1935–1957.
5. Prime ministers—Canada—Biography. I. Title. II. Series.

FC621.P4C64 2008   971.064'3092   C2008-902630-6

Visit the Penguin Group (Canada) website at **www.penguin.ca**

Special and corporate bulk purchase rates available; please see
www.penguin.ca/corporatesales or call 1-800-810-3104, ext. 477 or 474

This book was printed on 30% PCW recycled paper

For Geoffrey Pearson, who knew who he was

CONTENTS

John Ralston Saul

How do civilizations imagine themselves? One way is for each of us to look at ourselves through our society's most remarkable figures. I'm not talking about hero worship or political iconography. That is a danger to be avoided at all costs. And yet people in every country do keep on going back to the most important people in their past.

This series of Extraordinary Canadians brings together rebels, reformers, martyrs, writers, painters, thinkers, political leaders. Why? What is it that makes them relevant to us so long after their deaths?

For one thing, their contributions are there before us, like the building blocks of our society. More important than that are their convictions and drive, their sense of what is right and wrong, their willingness to risk all, whether it be their lives, their reputations, or simply being wrong in public. Their ideas, their triumphs and failures, all of these somehow constitute a mirror of our society. We look at these people, all dead, and discover what we have been, but also what we can be. A mirror is an instrument for measuring ourselves. What we see can be both a warning and an encouragement.

These eighteen biographies of twenty key Canadians are centred on the meaning of each of their lives. Each of them is very different, but these are not randomly chosen great figures. Together they produce a grand sweep of the creation of modern Canada, from our first steps as a democracy in 1848 to our questioning of modernity late in the twentieth century.

All of them except one were highly visible on the cutting edge of their day while still in their twenties, thirties, and forties. They were young, driven, curious. An astonishing level of fresh energy surrounded them and still does. We in the twenty-first century talk endlessly of youth, but power today is often controlled by people who fear the sort of risks and innovations embraced by everyone in this series. A number of them were dead—hanged, infected on a battlefield, broken by their exertions—well before middle age. Others hung on into old age, often profoundly dissatisfied with themselves.

Each one of these people has changed you. In some cases you know this already. In others you will discover how through these portraits. They changed the way the world hears music, thinks of war, communicates. They changed how each of us sees what surrounds us, how minorities are treated, how we think of immigrants, how we look after each other, how we imagine ourselves through what are now our stories.

You will notice that many of them were people of the word. Not just the writers. Why? Because civilizations are built around many themes, but they require a shared public language. So Laurier, Bethune, Douglas, Riel, LaFontaine, McClung, Trudeau, Lévesque, Big Bear, even Carr and Gould, were masters of the power of language. Beaverbrook was one of the most powerful newspaper publishers of his day. Countries need action and laws and courage. But civilization is not a collection of prime ministers. Words, words, words—it is around these that civilizations create and imagine themselves.

The authors I have chosen for each subject are not the obvious experts. They are imaginative, questioning minds from among our leading writers and activists. They have, each one of them, a powerful connection to their subject. And in their own lives, each is engaged in building what Canada is now becoming.

That is why a documentary is being filmed around each subject. Images are yet another way to get at each subject and to understand their effect on us.

There has not been a biographical project as ambitious as this in a hundred years, not since the Makers of Canada series. And yet every generation understands the past differently, and so sees in the mirror of these remarkable figures somewhat different lessons.

What strikes me again and again is just how dramatically ethical decisions figured in their lives. They form the backbone of history and memory. Some of these people, Big Bear, for example, or Dumont, or even Lucy Maud Montgomery, thought of themselves as failures by the end of their lives. But the ethical cord that was strung taut through their work has now carried them on to a new meaning and even greater strength, long after their deaths.

Each of these stories is a revelation of the tough choices unusual people must make to find their way. And each of us as readers will find in the desperation of the Chinese revolution, the search for truth in fiction, the political and military dramas, different meanings that strike a personal chord. At first it is that personal emotive link to such figures which draws us in. Then we find they are a key that opens the whole society of their time to us. Then we realize that in that 150-year period many of them knew each other, were friends, opposed each other. Finally, when all these stories are put together, you will see that a whole new debate has been created around Canadian civilization and the shape of our continuous experiment.

What always strikes me about Lester Pearson is his remarkable self-confidence—his and that of his band of friends who believed that Canada had to change. He instinctively understood that the real country was not being served or expressed by the system of leftover colonial habits which was still in place. What had to change was how we organized our society, how we projected justice among ourselves, how we explained and presented ourselves to ourselves, how we dealt with the rest of the world. In many ways, his five tempestuous, revolutionary years as prime minister remind me of the LaFontaine and Baldwin government in the middle of the nineteenth century. The country was somehow liberated by the mix of social improvements and political modernization.

Andrew Cohen knows as much about our life as a country in the larger world as anyone. He has thought deeply about how Canada should function at home and abroad. Here, he unleashes a charged portrait of the man who for two decades was the best-known Canadian in the world and one of the pivotal figures of our country's existence.

CHAPTER ONE

The Making of Mike

A little surprise awaits visitors by the back stairs on the second floor of Laurier House in Ottawa. In the Second Empire home of Sir Wilfrid Laurier and Mackenzie King, now a national historic site, they discover a small shrine to Lester Bowles Pearson. The strange thing is that Pearson never lived here. After his death, the archivists suggested there was room "for another Liberal prime minister in Laurier House" and asked the family for some of his mementoes. They used these to turn the servants' quarters into a replica of the study Pearson used in retirement. "We agreed that these things were part of Canadian history and the public should be able to see them," said Maryon Pearson, his widow, when she opened the study in 1974. It was to remain at Laurier House until a permanent home could be found. None was, and the exhibition is still here.

It helped that Pearson lived in a time of gifts rather than gift cards. Words were etched on silver rather than sent into cyberspace. It also helped that this *homme du monde* who had been everywhere seemed to keep everything—bowls, plaques, trophies, cups, medals, ribbons, photographs, cartoons, ceremonial keys, baseball bats, lacrosse rackets, even his diplomatic gold braid and blue uniform and the red-and-white robes he wore receiving one of his forty-nine honorary degrees. In the centre of the room is his unadorned desk and swivel chair from the basement of 541 Montagu Place in Rockcliffe Park, where he moved in 1968. Pearson's study has none of the solemnity of King's sanctum sanctorum on the floor above. No panelled Georgian library of pedestals, portraits, tapestries, leather wingback chairs, and crystal decanters here. This is Mike's Place: a sofa with throws, a wooden rocking chair, a metal globe, and a hand-hooked woven carpet in the design of the flag of Canada. The fraying, faux red brick is falling away in places. Behind the desk hangs a painting of the church in southern Ontario where Pearson's father was pastor and an outsize aerial photograph of Expo 67. With a walnut-veneer television console and an orange shag carpet, this could be a man-cave in any suburban bungalow, *circa* 1972.

Here are hints of the man's character: modesty, simplicity, curiosity, ambition. Here are the entrails of his experience in school, sports, the academy, diplomacy, government. What we don't know, a wall of photographs shows us:

Pearson as a baby in 1899, as a groom at his double wedding in 1925, as a grandfather with his brood in 1964. Pearson as statesman at the General Assembly; Pearson as Nobel Laureate in Oslo; Pearson as newly elected leader at the 1958 Liberal Party National Convention. Pearson with Sir Winston Churchill, Nikita Khrushchev, Louis St. Laurent, Dwight Eisenhower, Queen Elizabeth, and so many others.

Best wishes from John F. Kennedy ("with appreciation for a fruitful visit"), who greeted him warmly at Cape Cod in 1963, relieved he wasn't John Diefenbaker. From Secretary of State Dean Acheson ("to Mike and Maryon, with esteem and affection founded in many years of friendship and work and play together? [sic]"), who would have less esteem for this "moralizing" Canadian's views on Korea in 1951. From Lyndon Johnson ("with very high regards"), which were less high when Pearson spoke out on Vietnam in 1965. From Charles de Gaulle ("very cordially from your loyal friend of Canada"), who was neither friendly nor loyal when he visited Montreal in 1967.

Tucked away in this dim, airless mansion of death masks, Ouija boards, crystal balls, and the echo of seances, where Laurier moved the year Pearson was born and where King lived until his death in 1950, visitors find the talismans and tokens of a dazzling seventy-five years. "I have been fortunate in all my lives," Pearson said as they were beginning to run out. "I've had almost as many as a cat." Those lives took him from the parsonages of small-town Ontario to the battlefields of Europe. They led him to Toronto, Chicago, and Oxford to study and work, to London, Geneva, Washington, and New York to address—and sometimes resolve—the vexing issues of his time. And then back home, to Ottawa and a long, fitful stewardship in politics, first in opposition, then in government, leading the country, making his mark. When he died in 1972, his body lay in state. A nation mourned. They buried him on a hilltop in a cold rain.

For all that, Lester Pearson is known only vaguely to Canadians today. Scores of schools, an international college, and the country's busiest airport may bear his name, but polls suggest that Canadians don't really know why. They may have a gauzy, faint notion of him as an angel of peace. That he fought in the Great War and represented Canada at the League of Nations and the United Nations, that he was the best-known Canadian in the world of his time, that he rebuilt the Liberal Party and led it back to power, that he governed Canada for five feverish years— of all this, they know little. That he developed peacekeeping, created the flag, enacted health care, and introduced bilingualism—all of which have come to define contemporary Canada—of that they may know even less, if anything at all.

For its own odd, inexplicable reasons, Laurier House does not publicize that Lester Pearson lives on its second floor. In a museum devoted exclusively to the memory of Laurier and King, he is seen as an interloper; there is no mention of him or his study anywhere (not on its signs, not in its literature, printed or electronic). It is as if he is here illegitimately, a squatter under the eaves who has overstayed his welcome, an embarrassment and a secret.

Fortunately, by now, his story is out.

AT THE BEGINNING, who could have known how it would end? The world in which Lester Bowles Pearson arrived on April 23, 1897, was thoroughly unlike the one he left three-quarters of a century later. "God was in His heaven and Queen Victoria on her throne," he wrote in *Mike*, the first of his three-volume memoir, published in 1972. "All was well. The Empire, on which a sun never dared to set, was being made mightier yet; Canada was about to enter the century that belonged to her." The year of his birth marked the Diamond Jubilee of Britain's longest-serving monarch, presiding over the greatest empire the world had ever known. There may have been rebellion in India and unrest in the Transvaal, but all was peaceful in Canada thirty years after Confederation. At the turn of the century, Canada was largely rural, conservative, white, Christian, and British. It had no national flag, no foreign ministry, no citizenship or other symbols of nationhood that would become the motifs of Pearson's thrusting generation. At the same time, a patriot could believe that the new century would belong to Canada, as Sir Wilfrid Laurier would muse in 1904. Although Canada had few people, it did have land, resources, and freedom. As we know, the century would turn out differently for Great Britain and Canada. While the British Empire would collapse, Canada would become a country in more than name. Burdened by its own peculiar pathologies, though, Canada would not own the century. In fact, after a near-death experience over Quebec in 1995, it was happy to survive it.

Pearson was born in Newtonbrook, a hamlet on Yonge Street, north of Toronto, on St. George's Day. His mother's forebears were the Bowles, who came to Canada from Ireland in the 1830s. His maternal grandfather, Thomas Bowles, was a Methodist preacher who served as reeve of his township. He ran twice provincially and once federally for the Liberal Party, narrowly losing each time. Pearson's maternal grandmother, Jane Lester, enchanted her young grandson. Despite the age difference of seventy years, there was an intimacy between them. His other grandparents were part Irish. The Pearsons were Tories and the Bowles were Liberals, each aggressively so.

In his memoir, Pearson described a wholesome childhood of duty, piety, and affection. He was "doubly and deeply blessed" in his parents. "There is nothing but joy and thanksgiving in my memory of two fine, saintly characters," he wrote. "It is not possible to assess, though it is to acknowledge, how much I owe to them." His father was Edwin Arthur Pearson, a Methodist preacher like his father. For him, though, there was no politics. A mild-mannered, unworldly man, he used persuasion rather than damnation. "He led his flock rather than harried it," observed Pearson. The citation accompanying an honorary doctorate from the University of Toronto in 1927 praises Reverend Pearson's "sanity of judgment ... and warmth of heart ... in a genial and winning personality." Pearson remembers most deeply his father's love of games, particularly baseball, after prayers on Sunday.

His mother was Annie Sarah Bowles. She was educated, had a talent for art, and was influential in her sons' lives. Pearson recalls how hard she worked and how often she was unwell in middle age (even though she lived to ninety-four).

In a tightly knit family, Pearson wrote, she was "its soul and its solace. She surrounded her children with a sense of security and love that had its greatest reward in their growth and their successes. She never failed us." Like his father, she had reserve, fortitude, and wisdom. She completed their partnership, her son said, as the minister's wife.

Lester was the second of three sons. Duke was three years older; Vaughan was a year younger. Their father's nomadic ministry took the family to live in Davisville, Aurora, Toronto, Peterborough, Hamilton, and Chatham. New places meant new friends. There was always a big house with a lawn for games. As a boy, Lester didn't mix it up. "I was more of a pacifier than a pugilist," he said.

For Pearson and his brothers, there were few baubles. Drink and tobacco were evil; cards, a byword for gambling, were disdained, as were movies. Girls were alien. The family was said to live in "genteel poverty," but his father's salary ($700 a year in 1900) was often supplemented. Lester won scholarships and had money for necessities, though he longed for a bicycle, a Boy Scout uniform, and tube hockey skates. Later, he sold newspapers, though he maintained, in a subtle swipe at the boasts of John Diefenbaker, that neither being a paperboy nor being born in a log cabin (Diefenbaker was, Pearson wasn't) was the *sine qua non* of political success.

Pearson excelled in school and at sports too, especially hockey, baseball, and lacrosse. Beyond that, there were books. He learned of Shakespeare through the popular *Lambs' Tales*, and read much of Dickens and some of Thackeray. The richly illustrated *History of the World* impressed him. His favourite was G.A. Henty, the British author of adventure stories for boys. In his day, Henty was a sensation, spinning romantic tales of derring-do against the great events of history. Henty began writing his books in the 1860s and was still producing them after Pearson was born. Forgotten today, they remained popular well into the early decades of the twentieth century. *The Dash for Khartoum, Through Russian Snows, Under Wellington's Command, With Wolfe in Canada*—these were what animated a boy. In a life that would take him along the creases of the map of the world, Pearson recalls that there was scarcely a place he visited that he had not been before with G.A. Henty.

By all accounts, Lester was the perfect child. He was usually obedient, as well as loyal, smart, and devout, despite having some doubts about the demands of faith. For a son of the manse, with limited means, growing up in Edwardian Ontario was idyllic. Wisdom was always conventional and unchallenged. Verities were verities, facts were facts. Little was questioned.

"The air was pure and the skies clear and blue," he said of parsonage life. The metaphor obtains; his disposition was sunny and his weather was fair. If he was given a licking or two by his father, he never resented it. His parents were forgiving and tolerant, knowing where their authority ended and their children's independence began. They also imparted some useful rules: *Be nice to people on the way up because you may meet them on the way down. Be a good boy. Keep your feet dry.* In war, politics, and life, these adages served him well. Young Lester suffered none of the agonies of some great men: no Oedipus complex, no middle-child syndrome, no sibling rivalry, no parental abuse. On his life's journey, he carried no emotional baggage. As Pearson put it later: "Growing was for me a healthy, happy and relatively untroubled process."

The biographer searches for clues in childhood to explain adulthood. John English, the esteemed historian who wrote *The Life of Lester Pearson*, his exhaustive, two-volume biography, notes that Pearson "was to lead an urban, secular and international life that carried him, by his own admission, far from his early days." True, as a collegian, Pearson didn't enter the clergy as his parents had hoped. He chose the ministry of public service over the ministry of God (as did two of his American contemporaries who were sons of clergymen,

Dean Acheson and John Foster Dulles). As a student, he slept late on Sundays and played pool; as an adult, he rarely attended church. He drank moderately and by mid-life was no sexual puritan. He retained few friends from childhood, and his relations with his brothers did not remain close. Still, these early days left their mark in other ways. The Canada of Pearson's childhood was English, not French; that solitude did not imprint itself upon the starched collars of Peterborough and Chatham. He didn't learn French, nor did he know much about Quebec.

His saintly parents gave him roots, as the expression goes, but they also gave him wings. He appreciated that—no more so than when he and his brothers went off to war. His mother and father taught him gratitude and humility, which is how he could enter a profession of egotists and remain down to earth. They taught him as well to appreciate money without revering it. They encouraged both scholarship and athletics, which would bring much pleasure. Philosophically, Pearson moved away from Methodism and shed his small-town conservatism. Still, years later, when he sat up late in colloquies trying to reconcile old enemies, he might well have drawn comfort from the cadence of those hymns and the soothing words of those homilies from the sunny Sundays of his childhood.

LESTER PEARSON WAS SIXTEEN when he entered Victoria College, a Methodist institution at the University of Toronto, in 1913. There was no debate about where he would go; his father had studied at Victoria, and his older brother, Duke, was already there. They would room together at Burwash Hall, which would shelter Lester from the temptations of Toronto the Good. The residence was new, built by the wealthy family of Vincent Massey, who was its dean. This would be the beginning of a long association between Pearson and Massey extending "from Burwash Hall to Rideau Hall," where Massey would reside as Governor General forty years later. Always more correct than warm, their relations were tested early. Massey wanted the neo-Gothic residence to reflect the spirit of Oxford, from which he had just returned. Pearson objected. He said Burwash Hall was founded in 1912, not 1412, that it was filled with Canadian boys, not English lads, and that it would have to develop its own traditions, not import them. When Massey insisted students wear gowns at dinner, Pearson and his classmates wore sweaters. A small act of defiance from a sixteen-year-old, to be sure, but it was not the last time Pearson would assert an independent view of Canada.

Pearson took to university. As a freshman, he played on college teams, made friends, and earned a first in modern history. He returned home for the summer and played more baseball. He didn't think much when Great Britain declared war on August 4, even though Canada, as a dominion of the Empire, was now at war too. The war was far away and, like all wars, it would be over by Christmas. There would be a Charge of the Light Brigade and a Battle of Trafalgar, he thought, and that would be that. He returned to university that fall, won second prize in an oratorical contest, lost a football championship when he fumbled the ball ("a nightmare mistake which haunted me for ages"), and returned home for Christmas. Reverend Pearson, a fervent patriot, was encouraging those of age to enlist, which did not yet include Lester.

To a naïve adolescent, the war was a flight of fancy. It promised excitement in distant lands. In the autumn of 1914, as Canada was raising an expeditionary force, Pearson saw upperclassmen enlist and immediately leave school, their belongings auctioned off in the common room with mock solemnity. His brother Duke soon joined, although he stood barely five feet tall. Lester marched and drilled in the uniform of the University Officers Training Corps, led by Vincent Massey, for whom he ran messages in a training exercise. Although underage, Pearson wanted to enlist and go overseas. Like other English Canadians, he was full of idealism. The cause was just, whatever it was. "War was still a romantic adventure," he recalled. "Our views were not yet contaminated by revelations of prewar political maneuvering by the European governments in the pursuit of power rather than principle. We had no realization yet of the carnage that would follow the use of modern mechanical instruments of destruction." It was settled, then, at least for him. He would fight.

THE GREAT WAR would bring Pearson injury, although less physical than psychological. It would make him more rueful and reflective. And it would give him a moniker for life. Sent to the quieter eastern front, he was spared the misery of the trenches. He did not take Vimy Ridge or hunker down at the Somme, like Duke, or advance at Passchendaele, like his younger brother, Vaughan. But he saw the war for the awful folly that it was. In public or private, he rarely discussed the war and never glorified it. If anything, he disparaged his military service with humour or sarcasm.

"I was in the library in 1915, studying a Latin poet, and all of a sudden I thought: 'War can't be this bad.' So I walked out and enlisted," he recalled. His decision was a little less spontaneous than that, though. He had wanted to join for months, feeling "a growing uneasiness" about studying while friends were fighting. "I began to feel that I too must go." When he learned there was a vacancy in the University of Toronto Hospital Unit, which would soon be going overseas, he responded enthusiastically. On April 23, 1915, his eighteenth birthday, he rushed down to a recruiting office and joined up.

He became Private Pearson, #1059, of the Canadian Army Medical Corps. He put on an ill-fitting uniform, returned to the library, gathered up Plautus and Terence, and began preparing to ship out three weeks later. He wrote his final examinations, got credit for his second year (and, subsequently, a third for overseas service), and boarded the train for Montreal and the boat to Europe. His parents saw him off at Union Station in Toronto. He would be gone for three years.

And so began this "great, unknown adventure" that would take Pearson across the Atlantic Ocean on a filthy, crowded troop ship. The quarters were cramped and the food inedible. He was homesick and seasick. It was "the worst week I had ever experienced," he wrote. Dreaming of Henty, Pearson fancied himself dodging danger as he swept up the wounded in no man's land and brought them through shot and shell to safety. He imagined winning the Victoria Cross. *With Pearson at Passchendaele! Under Pearson's*

Command! But Henty was long dead and so were his Victorian heroes. Rather than carrying soldiers out of harm's way, Pearson began life in the army as an orderly, carrying bedpans.

The war did not come immediately. His wrenching transatlantic voyage ended in England, where he spent three months based at a camp hospital. Pearson discovered the London that he had read about, and he thrilled to its history and art. On the day a letter arrived telling him that he had won the Regent's Prize for the best English essay, on Tennyson, he was summoned by a sour sergeant suffering from lumbago. Our dreamy muse was ordered to wash the man's backside.

He was developing a distaste for imperial hauteur ("I began to hate class distinctions more than ever") and a defiance of military regimen; sailing to the eastern front, he and others in his company refused to parade naked on deck, where the British planned on hosing them down like packhorses. He was punished but continued to maintain that it was unbecoming to "my dignity as a recent Canadian civilian." He was asserting himself and learning the ragged ways of the world beyond Chatham. For instance, he saw nothing wrong with ameliorating his lowly situation by helping himself, if possible, to culinary delicacies "lost" in transit.

Despite these little rebellions, when his ship stopped in Alexandria, the wanton behaviour of Australian soldiers "shocked" this innocent Methodist.

FINALLY, IN OCTOBER 1915, Pearson landed in Salonica, the ancient city of Macedonia. There, on a muddy Balkan plain, he and his fellow stretcher-bearers—who at first had no stretchers—brought out the wounded Tommies and tended to them in a hospital tent. He recalls the cries of pain, the boom of guns, the struggling in the mud. In November, they suffered the worst blizzard in memory. Soldiers were still wearing tropical uniforms, as if this were the balmy Mediterranean. The days were long. For recreation, Pearson played soccer and ground hockey. There was the occasional respite at the Splendid Palace Hotel. Some of his friends were more adventurous, he recalls, implying they went looking for women. Not the reverend's son, though.

Salonica (now part of Greece) was the calmer theatre of the First World War. The Balkans escaped the wasting warfare of the Western Front, but the situation was, nevertheless, awful. Lashed by rain and sleet, caked in mud, chilled by the cold, and threatened by a cocktail of diseases including pneumonia, dysentery, typhus, malaria, and blackwater fever, Private Pearson lost his appetite for this inglorious exercise. "War in all its hideousness was revealed, and my last illusions of its adventure and its romance were destroyed," he wrote.

But for all that, Pearson wasn't miserable. Not at all. He was thriving. The enterprise may no longer have been romantic but it was still novel. Perhaps this is where his remarkable resiliency—which sustained him in political defeat—first showed itself. There were reasons for his good cheer. First, he was "invincibly" healthy. In a war in which half the troops came down with malaria or those other ill-nesses, he was strangely immune. The boy whose mother thought he would be sent home the moment he got his feet wet had not as much as a sniffle during those months. Second, he found himself a "cushy job" as quartermaster. This got him out of the hospital and the operating tent, where he'd once fainted at the sight of blood. Third, he was exhilarated by the camaraderie. His war, while it was not what he thought it would be, wasn't that bad, actually. He had good friends, good fun, good food.

Yet Pearson felt guilty. He had it too easy. He knew well how dreadful things were in France—Duke would soon be wounded at the Somme—but he wanted to go anyway. For all the talk about this war's hideousness, he craved more of it. His boyish instinct for adventure—or maybe his adult belief in service—impelled him to seek a transfer to another theatre. It wasn't easy, so he telegraphed his father in September 1916, asking for help. Ed Pearson spoke to General Sam Hughes, a fellow Methodist, who gave a perfunctory order: "Send Private Pearson back to England at once." It ruffled feathers, and it took time. In March 1917, he left for England, now an acting corporal, though with no increase in pay.

Some men tried to use their influence to avoid the war. But here was Pearson, not yet twenty years old, having spent almost two years in the mud and blood, pulling strings to *get in* the fight. Although he had been wanting to enter the Royal Flying Corps ever since he had once flown as an observer on a reconnaissance flight over enemy territory in the Balkans, he returned to England to secure an officer's commission in the infantry. He was sent to train at the University of Oxford, where he spent a blessed interlude while the slaughter worsened across the Channel. For a while, his war turned rosy. He joined a high-spirited company of Australians, New Zealanders, and South Africans, who were thrilled to be in that exquisite city. Their platoon commander was the gifted Robert Graves, who would write the trenchant anti-war memoir *Goodbye to All That* and become Pearson's lifelong friend. Of course, there were sports.

Pearson won a prize for throwing a cricket ball and breaking a record, a feat that earned him a mention in *The Times* (London). He was dispatched to the 4th Canadian Reserve Battalion, where Duke had also been reassigned. They trained for three months as infantry officers. Years later, Pearson recalled an address to the troops by Sir Arthur Currie, the commander of the Canadian Corps. Currie warned two or three times that "some of you will not come back," and young Pearson, so green in khaki, was certain that Currie was staring at him when he said it. But Pearson was not going to go, after all. The Royal Flying Corps needed pilots and he was asked to join. Finally, he was where he wanted to be.

The training was absurdly short. A year was compressed into six weeks, which may explain why pilots were dropping out of the sky. One day, Pearson's instructor hopped out of the plane on the runway and told him to fly by himself. His first solo flight came in a Graham White "Pusher"—a glorified box kite. He went up easily, stayed up confidently, and came down crudely. He liked flying. For a while he even allowed himself to believe that he was meant to be a flyer. Had Henty had an aviator as hero, it would surely have been him! Certainly Pearson looked the part. In a glamorous photograph of himself at flight school, he is clad in thick gloves, woollen cap, high boots, and a full-length leather greatcoat falling below his knees, collar high, belted at the waist. He leans against his airplane, a flimsy contraption of wire, canvas, struts, and a ninety-horsepower engine. One arm is cocked at his waist, the other rests upon the plane. He gazes ahead, benignly, serenely, contemplating a limitless horizon. *Lord of the Air? Master of the Skies?*

Ultimately, the most important thing Pearson got from flight training was a new name. The squadron commander thought that the name Lester wasn't fierce enough for a fighter pilot and arbitrarily decided to call him Mike. "The name stuck," Pearson recalled, "and I was glad to lose Lester." From then on he was Mike. The name became so familiar that it became the title of Pearson's memoirs.

On a later training flight, things went awry and he made a crash landing. He was not badly hurt—some bruises and scratches—but he spent a few days recovering near London and then had a night on the town, which did prove harrowing. During an air-raid blackout, a bomb went off a halfmile away. He got off a bus on Edgware Road and stepped in front of another speeding toward him without running lights. He was hit and knocked cold. Bystanders thought this teetotaller laid out on the sidewalk was a drunk, which amused Pearson, who called himself "probably the purest soldier in all the allied or enemy forces!" He ended up in hospital, then stayed with American friends in London and awaited new orders. That was that. His season as soldier had come to an unceremonious end.

Here, though, in the last theatre of Pearson's war, the story becomes deeply affecting. It is also mysterious. As he recovered in hospital from the leg and head wounds he suffered in the bus accident, Pearson had six weeks to reflect on what was happening in France and Belgium, on the meaning of this ghastly enterprise that had drawn a fresh-faced innocent across the ocean and offered him up to the machinery of death. Convalescence brought clarity. Of this bittersweet interval he said, "It was then that I became an adult." Talking to Clifford Hames, a fellow Canadian in flying school, he searched for answers. "We spent hours trying to get some understanding of what we were being asked to do; to bring some reason to the senseless slaughter. For what? King and country? Freedom and democracy? These words sounded hollow now in 1918 and we increasingly rebelled against their hypocrisy." Here was a soldier's despair. Historian C.P. Champion says Pearson did not become disillusioned with the Great War until much later, when the anti-war tracts, such as *Goodbye to All That*, began to appear. But the mood of his memoir and his letters suggest he already had deep reservations when he was in England.

Pearson, who was not given to great intimacy, allowed that he grew closer to Hames than to anyone else in his life beyond his family. In those anxious days, they talked and talked with a heavy sense of fatalism. Their generation was lost. The fighting would continue. They would join it. They would not survive it. But in March, Pearson learned he'd be invalided home. On April 6, he landed in Canada. On April 25, Hames died in France.

Here Pearson's war ends. A medical board in Canada recommended that he be discharged. When Pearson was asked pointedly by a superior whether he wanted to remain in the service, he said yes; later, he asked to go with the Canadian Expeditionary Force to Siberia. Although he had wanted to come home for a spell, he had mixed feelings about leaving the military. He had written his parents before his return from England that but for them, he didn't think he should leave. After three years of active duty, as a soldier who had volunteered, he could have presumably quit then with honour. He didn't. Duty mattered.

But Pearson doesn't tell the whole story of his last days in uniform. Nor do the biographies or the obituaries. The fullest explanation comes from John English, who pieces together letters, reports, and newspaper clippings and concludes that Pearson was suffering from neurasthenia, what English calls "a shattering of nerves." His condition was attributed to the plane crash rather than the embarrassing traffic accident. It seemed like a nervous breakdown. Pearson was suffering the strain of three years of worry. Many others were too. But like other forms of mental incapacity, this affliction was simply not discussed. Certainly Pearson, an avatar of Victorian restraint, did not talk about it.

Nor would he discuss his war. His generation wasn't given to that kind of soulful introspection (nor were veterans of the next world war). No prime minister served in the army as long as Pearson did. John Diefenbaker was discharged after sixteen months; Pierre Trudeau chose not to serve at all in the Second World War. It is possible, though not obvious, that the Great War made Pearson more cautious about the use of force and gave him credibility later as a conciliator. Other politicians of his era would invoke the war. "I have seen war. I hate war," said Franklin Delano Roosevelt in 1936, though he had never served in uniform. Pearson didn't talk that way. Politically, he wasn't a war profiteer. "I got hurt before I got a chance to get killed—that's about what it amounts to," he said.

In 1967, before another audience of veterans marking the fiftieth anniversary of the Battle of Vimy Ridge, he allowed himself a brief reminiscence of his life as Private #1059 L.B. Pearson. He mentioned his two years of "obscure service" in the Balkans and then reprised the much more celebrated battle at Vimy, wondering, as if he had sat out the war as a conscientious objector, "who am I to repeat it to those who were the story … ?" The war was simply not part of his life's narrative. In the 1962 election, when a fellow Liberal on the stump enthused about Pearson's "distinguished" war record, Pearson gently corrected him.

"My war service was just about as undistinguished as it could be," he said. "I managed to stay alive."

CHAPTER TWO

The Happiest Years

After his season of war and adventure, returning to school was not terribly attractive for Lester Pearson. There was that restlessness that comes from surviving a harrowing passage. There were also those shattered nerves and loss of self-confidence. Mike was not a Henty hero. He talks little about his homecoming in his memoir. Medical reports suggest that he was pale, jittery, and suffered nightmares long after he had returned to Toronto and the war ended on November 11, 1918. Having been awarded his third year for military service, Pearson returned to Victoria College at the University of Toronto the following January for his fourth and final year. He was allowed to complete it in a single term. He played football and hockey that autumn and winter and enjoyed both immensely. He passed his examinations with honours in history (mostly, he said, due to a kindly examiner understanding a veteran's situation) and graduated with a Bachelor of Arts on June 5, 1919. He was twenty-two years old, a jaded warrior, a desultory scholar, and a growing skeptic.

What now? Where would he fit in postwar Canada? He thought he'd have a career in law, and began his articles at McLaughlin, Johnson, Moorehead and Sinclair, as apprentice lawyers did then. But he found the prospect of contracts, torts, and clerical work "abhorrent." He decamped after one week. Baseball was more appealing. In the summer of 1919, Pearson joined the semi-professional Guelph Maple Leafs as infielder while punching a clock at Partridge Tire and Rubber Company. He was good at baseball. Years later, when he was a diplomat of renown, he was asked what he had that his colleagues didn't. He replied that he was the only diplomat who was paid to play baseball. Unfortunately, baseball offered no future. So that autumn he approached his uncle, Edson White, an executive of Armour and Company of Chicago, the large meatpacking concern. White had admired the Pearson brothers for going to war when America was neutral, and he promised them help on their return. True to his word, Uncle Edson found Pearson a job at the company's subsidiary in its stockyards in Hamilton, Ontario.

When Pearson reported for work in September 1919, he was assigned to the sausage department. The foreman carefully explained the process to his new trainee, L.B. Pearson, B.A. Just as he had imagined doing something more glamorous in the army than washing men's backsides, Pearson had hoped for something more challenging in business than pouring meat into sausage casing. From stretcher-bearer to sausage-stuffer. Cynical he was not, but Mike could be forgiven for thinking that he had simply exchanged one abattoir for another.

Yet he didn't quit. He played hockey in Hamilton and enjoyed the company of fellow factory hands, showing again his ability to get along with people and overcome disappointment. When he finally got to the Windy City in February 1920, expecting a promotion, he learned that he would be a clerk. Once again, he worked hard, made new friends, and enjoyed a city careering into the tumultuous Twenties. He also realized that the meatpacking business wasn't for him. "I've got a job that stinks," he sighed. It wasn't just the work. "I will never be satisfied making material success my whole aim[;] not that I don[']t love comfort & all the advantages money can buy," he wrote his parents on February 3, "but it doesn't satisfy everything[;] a business career will never make me really contented." Pearson decided that what he really wanted was to study at Oxford and teach in Toronto. White agreed, concluding that business wasn't for him, anyway. He offered his nephew some parting advice that Mike always remembered: find satisfying work and stick with it, wherever it may lead.

And he decided something else. He did not "want to live in Chicago or indeed in any part of the United States for the rest of my life. In short, I wanted to remain a Canadian in Canada...." Whether this was an epiphany born of the blood-stained stockyards or a Methodist's revulsion to a materialistic America, it is pivotal to his personal development. In the letter to his parents he is clear: "I want to live in my own country and doing the work I am called for." Here was a young man of promise in a great metropolis. He could have made his career there. Many of his contemporaries did, which is why emigration from Canada to the United States swelled in the 1920s. Instead, Pearson would follow Mackenzie King, O.D. Skelton, and Stephen Leacock, who had gone to Chicago and then returned home.

Was this attachment to Canada a product of the war? Possibly. John English believes that Pearson became more aware of his identity as a Canadian in Europe. While he remained a loyal British subject—Canada would not have its own citizenship until 1947—and he admired all things British, he was more committed to Canada when he returned. But this was a subtle recognition—it wasn't a Vimy moment. Pearson didn't muse much about his embryonic

Canadianism either. While Vimy is considered a crucible of national identity, he didn't mention the battle as a personal touchstone. Later, he cast Vimy in the predictable words leaders uttered then and now on its anniversary in April. "Vimy was more than a battle," Pearson said in 1967. "It has become for Canada a symbol. It is a symbol ... of the courage and sacrifice of Canadian men."

IF THE WAR SHARPENED Pearson's nationalism, it whetted his wanderlust. Loyal as he was to Canada, he sought the exotica of Away throughout his life. He always knew that he was a Canadian, and his periods of work or study outside Canada would be ephemeral. He didn't want to emigrate. But his nationalism was neither petty, resentful, nor parochial; it was broad and optimistic.

Pearson had promised himself that if he survived the war, he would return to Oxford, where he had had that lovely respite in 1917. The problem was that he didn't have the money. Here again, his instinct and industry made the difference. He had heard about the Massey Foundation Fellowship (he was ineligible for the Rhodes Scholarship because he was a graduate), which paid for graduate studies abroad. He applied and was interviewed by Vincent Massey, his former don at Victoria College and a former Oxonian. Massey liked him (presumably forgetting Pearson's resistance to dressing for dinner) and fixed up the fellowship. Bartlett Brebner, an army friend who had recently graduated from St. John's College, arranged for his admission to that illustrious institution. An excited Pearson sailed for England in 1921.

Oxford was a sweet sojourn. "Seldom are expectations so completely fulfilled as were those of my two years at Oxford," Pearson recalls in his memoir. "I loved it all...." For this student of British history, raised on the stories and characters of *Boy's Own Annual*, Oxford was both familiar and exotic. "It became a kind of a dream," he told biographer John Beal in the 1960s. "If I could only get over to Oxford, and experience that kind of life." But Pearson was more worldly than the milk-fed naïf who had arrived in England in 1915.

Medieval and brooding, Oxford after the Great War was immortalized in Evelyn Waugh's elegiac novel *Brideshead Revisited*. It was ancient and ivied, its worn streets and shaded paths echoing with the whispers of history, its skyline etched by spires. Here was the nursery of the postwar generation, a theatrical cast of sweatered and tweedy fops, cads, dandies, poseurs, strivers, ne'er-do-wells, homosexuals, sybarites, and aristocrats. Here were also revolutionaries, idealists, and intellectuals. Some of the Canadians would stay on in

Britain. Others would return to Canada and make their mark in politics, science, arts and letters. Many would become diplomats. Roland Michener, who had a brilliant career in public service, offered a characteristic description of Pearson in 1921: "Mike was a delightful companion and personality. He was informal, approachable, not aged by his war experience particularly. He was sort of carefree."

Although Pearson would later spend five years teaching in a university, he was never a serious scholar. Not for him the sepulchral carrels or the dusty shelves; he didn't have the solitary nature that scholarship demands. At Oxford he read modern history. The gentlemanly pace suited him. He met his tutor twice a week and wrote essays for discussion by the fire, wreathed in tobacco smoke. His favourite tutor was W.C. Costin, who would become president of St. John's College and a lifelong friend. Proud of his famous intellectual progeny, Costin cabled Pearson in the 1960s: "With Dean Rusk (St. John's) Secretary of State in Washington, Michael Stewart (St. John's) Foreign Secretary in London, and Mike Pearson (St. John's) Prime Minister in Canada, all's well with the world."

All was well with Mike's world. By 1921, the war was now behind him; he had shaken its phantoms and shadows. He took naturally to the joys and eccentricities of life at

Oxford: lunch around the ancient fireplace with his fellow bedders, served by a scout; dinner in cap and gown at high table; witty toasts at the King Charles' Club; silly debates at the Sophists Club; white flannels and green blazers at the Archery Club. But Mike Pearson was not the aesthete Charles Ryder or the dyspeptic Sebastian Flyte of Brideshead. Still a teetotaller, he declined champagne and sherry. And he eschewed romance. He drank most lustily from the well of sport, healthy and wholesome as it was. Pearson tried out for everything at Oxford but rowing. He picked up rugger quickly and played competently. He was a star in lacrosse, the highest scorer in the South of England League, and he was invited to join a tour of eastern American colleges during the Easter holidays in 1922. But his big thing was hockey. The Oxford team was "a Canadian show" comprised of expatriates who had played senior college hockey. Pearson played defence. The team was so strong it beat Cambridge 27–0. At Christmas they played in a hotel in Switzerland, and Pearson also played for the Swiss national team and competed in the European championships. They called him Herr Zigzag.

Sports preoccupied Pearson—too much so for Costin's liking. To show his bona fides, Pearson spent a summer studying German with Michener in Heidelberg, the alpine town in Bavaria. In inflationary Weimar Germany, he lived like a pasha; dinner with a bottle of champagne cost a quarter. By his second year, Pearson studied harder, spurred by an offer to teach in the Department of History at the University of Toronto if he got a first in his final examinations. He got a second, but the offer was honoured nonetheless, and he declined the option of staying a third year at Oxford.

Pearson was blissfully detached at Oxford. The upheaval of postwar Europe—strikes in Britain, rebellion in Ireland, revolution in Germany—swirled about him, unmentioned in his memoirs. "I had no desire as an overseas scholar to become concerned with British social change or political activity," he recalled. So Pearson did not join demonstrations in the streets of London or Manchester. Yet he did write dispatches at $10 apiece for the *Christian Guardian*, interpreting Europe through the eyes of a twenty-six-year-old Canadian. He was developing an interest in the world and, John English suggests, an early belief in the international community. He remained an ardent anglophile.

Beyond an education, Pearson drew two things from Oxford. One was that he rubbed shoulders with the men who would run the world, such as Harold Macmillan, the future British prime minister, and Gladwyn Jebb, the future diplomat (Dean Rusk and Michael Stewart, whom Costin

:arson). More important,
ere, such as Michener;
e minister; and Graham
oadcasting. There were
who attended Oxford
ng, Norman Robertson,
orge Ignatieff, Douglas
the nucleus of Canada's
ates would also shape
n, the novelist; Frank
rians; David Lewis, the
tutionalist. Pearson had
any friends at Oxford.

Oxford also gave Pearson a greater sense of nationalism. The idea of Canada as a distinct, autonomous entity, which had begun to take root in his mind in Europe and sprout in Chicago, bloomed in England. He noted wryly that, upon arriving at Oxford, he wanted to make a good impression on the head porter "by convincing him that, while a colonial, I was a well-bred and cultivated one. Above all, I must not be mistaken for an American." It was Oxford in particular that deepened Pearson's consciousness of Canada and that of many of his illustrious compatriots who returned home to shape the country in the middle decades of the century. To

J.W. Pickersgill, the veteran politician who served in Pearson's cabinet, Oxford was "the greatest of all schools of English-Canadian nationalism." Pearson reflected the same feeling in 1940: "I have more than once been struck by the fact that some of our most ardent nationalists are Oxford graduates who find it quite easy to reconcile their Canadian nationalism with a devotion to Oxford...."

Because Pearson had been increasingly aware of his attachment to Canada before Oxford, there is no sign of an epiphany there. It just seemed to grow. We do know that if Pearson returned more of a nationalist, it wasn't because he was treated as a coolie by Britons. He was never humiliated or patronized. In fact, Pearson was so much a creature of Oxford that Gladwyn Jebb called him "one of us." In a sense, he was. While many of the Canadians socialized exclusively with one another—a natural instinct among expatriates anywhere—Pearson mixed not only with them (he was president of the Colonial Club) but also with Britons and others (he was vice-president of the King Charles' Club). No wonder Pearson called Oxford "the happiest years of my life."

But his time at Oxford also deepened his affection for Britain. Historian C.P. Champion argues engagingly that while Pearson and his ilk may have returned with a heightened consciousness of Canada, they absorbed a good deal of Britannica too. Perhaps so. After Oxford, Pearson called himself a "British-Canadian conservative" with no party allegiance. He liked the monarchy and other institutions. How this Britishness actually manifested itself, though, is uncertain. Hume Wrong may have bought his suits from a Savile Row tailor who visited Ottawa every year to take orders from a rumpled mandarinate, but he never affected an English accent or adopted English manners. Pearson may have called London his favourite city, but he could never retire there as former prime minister R.B. Bennett did. Much as Pearson was a product of Britain, he was never its captive. This is why he could break with Britain over Suez (which greatly disturbed Michener and Charles Ritchie, who called it "the best bet in a bad world.") Pearson knew who he was. In the end, the greatest expression of his nationalism at Oxford was his decision to leave England and make his career in Canada.

THERE WAS A REASON TO RETURN: he had a job. In 1923, Pearson assumed the lectureship in modern history he'd been offered at the University of Toronto. He would also become a don in Middle House at Burwash Hall. In the way that one thing seamlessly followed another in his life, opportunity knocked and Pearson answered. He was pleased to have the job he had imagined when he left Chicago for Oxford. He was twenty-six years old and earning a respectable $2,000 a year. His course was set. "I expected to spend at least the next quarter century teaching history to the students of my old university, with forays into related activities," he recalled. "I knew that I would never become a cloistered scholar, but I did not know where one of these forays was to lead me."

Those forays would begin in the groves of academe. Teaching would be the first rung as he bounded up the ladder of ambition. Step by step he followed a course that would end, forty years later, at the doorway of 24 Sussex Drive. Yet becoming prime minister was never an early aspiration for Pearson. Unlike Brian Mulroney, who told classmates that he would be prime minister, or Pierre Trudeau, who told his diary that "I must be a great man," Pearson had no such impulse. "When I look back on my career, the most amazing thing is that things just happened," he reflected after he became prime minister. "I was always alert for any opportunities or responsibilities or interesting work, but if I didn't take it on, it didn't worry me. I'd do something else. I have never hewn to any particular line. It was only pressure, really, that got me into this. I was always taught as a boy in my family not to run away from anything. If you were convinced you ought to do it, try to do it."

If his ascent wasn't planned, though, it wasn't accidental either. Pearson was like the goaltender who makes save after extraordinary save; while he doesn't always know where the puck is, he senses where it is likely to go. And so he goes there, positioning himself to succeed. He situates himself. Pearson made friends, worked hard, created options. It isn't surprising that offers came to him. When they did, he knew when to say yes and when to say no. With this studied insouciance, he made himself a beneficiary of opportunity. He was fortune's child.

Like almost everything he did after stuffing sausages in Hamilton, Pearson enjoyed teaching. His field was European and British history. It was then that he became seriously interested in international affairs, contemplating the sad train of events that had led to the Great War—and the responsibility of countries such as Canada. "I decided that those responsibilities could not be discharged until Canada had full control of her own policies," he wrote. After he came home, he became "more and more liberal and nationalist, though far from a radical in my views." Pearson was joined at the University of Toronto by like-minded colleagues, including Hume Wrong, George Glazebrook, Frank Underhill, and

Donald Creighton, with whom Pearson would fall out years later. They were also rethinking Canada's place in the new world. Pearson's thoughts were beginning to form. Says John English: "Mike returned to Toronto bearing opinions that were a curious blend of Canadian nationalism, traditional British imperialism, and nascent internationalism." But none was extreme—no Fabian socialist or communist he—and none found expression in politics.

As always, he got a lot of enjoyment from sports. In addition to teaching and conducting tutorials, he played squash and tennis and coached football, hockey, and basketball at Victoria College. Then he moved on to coaching the university teams. Professor Pearson always found the time; he said that it took "only two or three hours a day." He loved competition and the collegiate life. His years in Toronto were among his richest, he recalled. So important were sports to Pearson that shortly after he announced that he was leaving teaching to join the government, he was invited to become director of athletics and head football coach at the university, with reduced teaching duties. Enamoured as he was of athletics, he was tempted but wisely decided that there were other playing fields to conquer.

Scholarship didn't move him. While he did publish occasional articles in newspapers and magazines and gave numerous speeches in his half-decade at the university, he never produced a scholarly article or book. Encouraged by his department head to write a history of the United Empire Loyalists, which might form the basis of a doctoral thesis, he went to Ottawa in the summer of 1926 to do research in the National Archives. But he was more interested in going to the House of Commons to watch the drama over Mackenzie King's government. He did little work that summer. It was Hume Wrong, Pearson's brilliant but truculent future colleague, who was the rising star on campus. "I quickly observed that Mike Pearson did not inspire anything like the admiration accorded Hume Wrong," recalled Paul Martin Sr., a student in those days, who, as a politician, did not inspire anything like the admiration accorded Pearson.

For Pearson, what was most memorable about his time at the University of Toronto was meeting Maryon Elspeth Moody of Winnipeg, the middle child of a doctor and a nurse. She was one of the students in his fourth-year course in European history. Half his students were women, all of them attractive. He remembers "one pretty dark-haired girl with a clear and enquiring mind" who stood out. They met soon after his arrival in 1923. Pearson said he was often accused of indecision in life—but he knew in four weeks he wanted to marry her. They became secretly engaged in the spring of 1924 and married the next year. In the careful prose of his memoir, Pearson speaks diffidently about their courtship, which took place while he was teaching her. Today a romance between professor and student would be considered risqué, if not scandalous. In the 1920s, it was strangely acceptable. Perhaps the fact that both Maryon and Mike were the God-fearing children of Methodists would ensure chastity. Who would know that Miss Moody, known as audacious and flirtatious, had tried the forbidden pleasures of liquor, cigarettes, cards, dancing, and, perhaps, sex too? If they had liaisons in the library, or stole kisses behind the bleachers, neither ever said. Whether he gave her an A for her coursework, he wouldn't quite admit that either. But their clandestine relationship—and an affair that he would have later in his marriage—suggests that Pearson, who had reached an age "well beyond the average for matrimony," as he put it, was less innocent than he seemed. And she too.

They were married in Winnipeg on August 22, 1925. They had a double wedding with Maryon's elder sister, Grace, who was marrying Norman Young. Maryon had wanted to elope, author Heather Robertson says, but Mike was more conservative and he didn't object to sharing the occasion. Maryon called his laconic wedding speech "the worst ever made by a bridegroom." Mike appreciated her "candid and loving frankness" and shrugged, as he did the rest of his life when his flinty wife unburdened herself. That autumn they began married life on the top floor of a Victorian house at 12 Admiral Road—now the home of Adrienne Clarkson, the former Governor General, and John Ralston Saul, the writer and editor of this series—in the Annex, a leafy neighbourhood near the university. Pearson was promoted from lecturer to assistant professor in 1926. They had their first child, Geoffrey Arthur Holland, in 1927. A daughter, Patricia Lillian, arrived in 1929.

In his memoir, Pearson speaks of Maryon reverentially. Whether he had regrets in forty-seven years of marriage, he never lets on. He salutes her as a dutiful wife who bore more than half the burden of their partnership, and he generously attributes his success to her. He apologizes for asking more of her than she expected when she married "a professor, to live the tranquil life on a university campus which most appealed to her." This is the lament often associated with Maryon, who made no secret of her distaste for public life. Her irascibility isn't a secret; she was said to have "the Moody temperament," and was notorious for jibes, retorts, and insults on appearance or comportment that wounded both her children and her grandchildren. Her unvarnished temperament made her terribly difficult, especially in old age.

It's unlikely, though, that Maryon would have been happy in the sedentary world of a professor's wife. In a letter to a friend in May 1924, she wrote: "I should love him to get into the diplomatic service some day—and be Ambassador somewhere—after all, why not dream? … I think we are both full of Ambition and we both believe in one another so thoroughly—I am quite sure he will do something big in the world some day!" Her words were not only prophetic (at the time, her fiancé was a professor and Canada still had no diplomatic service), they were revealing. Maryon's ambitions for herself as a writer came to nothing ("Maryon never worked a day in her life!" her brother Herbert told Heather Robertson), but she did have hopes for her husband beyond the academy. And if she famously said that behind every successful man is a surprised woman, he surely couldn't have been a surprise to her. She knew that Mike was a striver who was going places, which is why she married him then and encouraged him later. No, she could not have been surprised by his subtle but sustained ambition, not really. Particularly not in 1928, when it would carry him to the next destination of desire.

CHAPTER THREE

The Loose-Jointed First Secretary

In 1925, Mackenzie King asked O.D. Skelton, a brilliant political scientist and the dean of arts at Queen's University, to become undersecretary of the Department of External Affairs. The department had been established in 1909 but was little more than an archive and post office. Because Canada was a dominion of the Empire, its foreign relations were within the family, so to speak. But after the Imperial Conference of 1926, things changed. Skelton, who believed that an autonomous Canada needed an autonomous diplomacy, was given a mandate to create a bona fide foreign service. A supreme talent scout, Skelton would recruit a corps of gifted practitioners. His standards were so exacting that only one person was hired in 1926 and five in 1927. Largely white and Protestant, they were generalists rather than specialists, who believed in the possibility of Canada. No colonials need apply.

In the spring of 1928, Mike Pearson applied. He had met Skelton by chance during his summer in Ottawa in 1926. Skelton told him he was looking for bright young men (women were not admitted until later) to fill the fledging department. There was an exchange of letters, and then in June Pearson spent three days writing the examinations for first secretary. He was offered the position. And so began a new chapter, which, like so many others in his eventful life, seemed to happen, unsought and unsolicited, leaving us to marvel at his superb timing and effortless ascent.

But it is mistaken to suggest, as biographer John Beal does, that "he took the examination more or less by request, without any real desire to enter the diplomatic service." Or that, as Pearson himself recalled in his memoir, he heard in the winter of 1927 that examinations were to be held in Ottawa for first and third secretary. John English finds that no examinations were scheduled. It appears that Pearson was intrigued about a service based on merit rather than patronage and wrote Skelton to ask about his prospects. Just as Pearson plays down his interest in going to Ottawa, he also plays down his ability. He placed first in that competition, beating Kenneth Kirkwood, who had once been Maryon's suitor. He also bested the formidable Norman Robertson, which he would remember thirteen years later when

Robertson was appointed undersecretary, a job Pearson felt should have been his.

Curious, these things. We know now that Lester Pearson was an inspired choice. He would rise from first secretary to counsellor to assistant undersecretary to minister to ambassador to undersecretary. His would be a singularly brilliant career in a service that John F. Kennedy and other foreigners in the 1950s would call the finest in the world, an accolade that, sadly, we no longer hear today. Yet Skelton didn't rhapsodize about Pearson in 1928. There is no sense of him discovering a star. Skelton found Professor Pearson "distinct" and "attractive" but agreed with Vincent Massey that "there was something curiously loose-jointed and sloppy about his [Pearson's] mental makeup which, as a matter of fact, is reflected in some measure in his physical bearing." There is also something condescending in Massey's oft-quoted assessment of Pearson. After all, wasn't he the star athlete who had just aced the test?

Starting on the ground floor of the Department of External Affairs meant working on the top floor of the East Block of the Parliament Buildings. Under the sloping, crenellated roof, Pearson sat cheek by jowl with the amiable Hugh Keenleyside, who had joined at the same time and would soon spend seven years in Japan. From their Gothic aerie, they could gaze down upon the greensward shaded by the Peace Tower. There they learned everything they needed to know about the foreign service. In time, their cramped quarters under the eaves became known as "the University of the East Block." The department would remain there until 1973, when it moved to a castellated new headquarters on Sussex Drive that would bear the name of that sloppy, loose-jointed first secretary in the attic.

Pearson reported for work in August 1928. He had been asked to hurry to Ottawa, and left Maryon to pack up kit and kin in Toronto. At first Pearson found the job "unde-manding" and "uninspiring." Then again, these were early days. The department had no minister—the prime minister filled that role until 1946—and no more than a dozen offi-cers in four legations around the world. Within twenty years, as the business of diplomacy took Pearson to swelling missions in London and Washington, External Affairs would become the high church of government, the aristocracy of the bureaucracy. Not immediately though. It would take time for Skelton's legion of bright young men from Oxford and Harvard to build their esteemed foreign service. It would take commitment from their political masters too, who sometimes wavered.

For the dominions, the trend was up and out, and in 1928, Canada was detaching itself from the Empire. An early step was the Paris Peace Conference of 1919, which Canada attended as an independent entity, with its own representative. Another was the Imperial Conference of 1926, which established co-operation among free governments. A third and decisive step was in 1931, when the Statute of Westminster allowed the dominions to conduct foreign policy. Pearson believed that this gave Canada full freedom of movement, though he was often frustrated with the reluctance of his government to exercise it. He applauded Mackenzie King's nationalism, which emboldened Canada to accept a (non-permanent) seat on the Council of the League of Nations in 1927, but wondered why Canada refused to say anything. "His attitude reflected a prominent but unhappy Canadian characteristic, a persistent depreciation of our own capacities," Pearson wrote of King. Pearson wanted Canada to assert itself. Making a bigger Canada became the mantra of his public life.

An early, temporary assignment brought him to Washington in the summer of 1929. The next winter he was sent to the London Naval Conference, where he talked about disarmament and reducing the navy (though Canada had only one ship). He learned the wiles of diplomacy and began to enjoy it. Curiously, his greatest contribution in his early years of public service was domestic. In 1930, R.B. Bennett and the Conservatives were elected. Pearson was a beneficiary. In the next five years, he was twice asked to assist the work of economic royal commissions. This taught him about the harsh realities of life during the Great Depression and introduced him to western Canada beyond Winnipeg. It didn't hurt his career either.

When Bennett needed a secretary to the Royal Commission on Grain Futures, which his government created in 1931, Skelton recommended Pearson. The commission held hearings and made recommendations in a seventy-two-page report that acknowledged "the very efficient help given by our secretary." Pearson made a larger contribution to the Royal Commission on Price Spreads and Mass Buying in 1934. According to one account by journalist Patrick Nicholson in 1968, unacknowledged in his memoirs, Pearson wanted the job badly and contrived mightily to land it. The job was demanding; he had to organize the research and writing of a comprehensive report—eventually totalling 449 pages—on the national economy. "Never ... did I work harder than on this assignment," he wrote of days that stretched to fourteen hours. "At the end I was completely exhausted." The commission recommended ways to reduce the concentration of corporate power in Canada. It was here that Pearson met Walter Gordon, a successful chartered accountant from Toronto who would become his friend and finance minister. As Gordon recalled, Pearson already showed the humour, tact, and dedication that ingratiated him to everyone.

For Pearson, the commission was an immersion in the modern economy. "If they wanted to educate somebody for a future job in politics they couldn't have done it better," he wrote. When later critics said that Pearson had been abroad too long to know Canada, they must have forgotten his experience here. His work at the commission also demonstrated his bountiful energy; Bennett told Parliament that Pearson was "on the verge of complete nervous breakdown because of the extra work he did...." Hard work would distinguish Pearson in his long career. That, and his versatility, reliability, and compatibility.

In appreciation, Bennett invited Pearson to accompany him on business to London. On the voyage Bennett asked Pearson to review his list of nominees for the Order of the British Empire (OBE). Pearson winced when he saw his own name; he knew Skelton would be uncomfortable with one of his officers receiving this kind of recognition. So Pearson craftily asked Bennett to reclassify his job and give him a raise of $25 a week, telling the prime minister: "You can't raise a family on an OBE!" An annoyed Bennett replied that if Pearson persisted he would not get the honour or the money. In the end, he got both. The coda: Pearson missed the investiture at Rideau Hall and received the award some time later, while he was playing tennis one Saturday. A car drove up and the secretary to the Governor General, whom Pearson knew well, got out. The man approached the wire fence and unceremoniously tossed over a small case. "Here's your OBE," he sniffed.

Pearson liked Bennett, who treated him as a protegé. He found Bennett "outgoing" and "straightforward" (unlike King). Bennett liked Pearson too. During the war, after the former prime minister had moved to the county of Surrey, west of London, he and Pearson would occasionally see each other. This warmth came naturally to Pearson, and people admired him for it.

IN 1935, Pearson was posted to London, his first overseas diplomatic assignment. Not only would he spend six years in "the only great city in the world fit to live in," he would have a bird's-eye view of the roiling events of that "low, dishonest decade." This was a formidable time for Pearson, who, at thirty-eight, was a veteran of seven years of varied and useful service. Beyond organizing two royal commissions, he had now attended several international conferences on disarmament and international security. This not only exposed him to the nuances of diplomacy, it deepened his belief that Canada needed an independent voice in the world.

He was dismayed that Canada would not support a proposal before the League of Nations to impose oil sanctions on Italy for invading Ethiopia. Under Dr. W.A. Riddell, Canada's permanent representative to the League, Canada had proposed the sanctions in committee. Bennett had approved them. But King, who succeeded Bennett in the autumn of 1935, worried about antagonizing Italy and repudiated them. Pearson, who was en route to his new position in London, was sent to replace Riddell in Geneva, where he was forced to remain silent at the conference. "I hated just to sit there and not have any views about anything," he complained. The next year, King told the House of Commons that repudiating the oil sanctions was right; had his government not done so, "the whole of Europe might be aflame today." The prime minister was comforted by that notion. Pearson, whose isolationist sentiments never ran as deep as those of Skelton or King, thought otherwise: "My own view is that the failure in 1935 of the members of the League of Nations, including Canada, to stand up to a single aggressor, had much to do with the world war in 1939." Watching the march to war was painful to Pearson, as it was to all the veterans of the Great War. June Rogers, the daughter of Hume Wrong, who was wounded at the Somme, said that nothing was more agonizing for her father than his enforced paralysis as permanent representative to the League of Nations during the Munich Crisis in 1938.

Given the gathering storm—and the failure of the civilized world to stop it—much of what preoccupied Pearson during his early days in London was trivial. His duties included handling the problems of émigrés to Canada, helping Canadians contact relatives fighting in the civil war in Spain, and writing reports to Ottawa that were ignored. When he began work at Canada House in October 1935, no one knew what he was to do. His title was political secretary. When that conflicted with the work of Georges P. Vanier, who was Massey's deputy, they worked out a modus operandi that left Pearson no title at all. There was no turf war here; gentlemen both, they agreed to divide responsibilities, and that was that. Pearson's main duty was to keep abreast of things at Whitehall in the Foreign and Dominions Office. This brought him in touch with counterparts who liked him and shared dispatches and gossip with him. He knew that Ottawa was keenly concerned that Canada maintain distance between itself and Britain. This policy of "no entan-glements" was devised to avoid compromising Canada's hard-won independence within the Commonwealth. "The concept of our 'empire' and 'our dominions' died hard in Britain," said Pearson, whose duty it was, among others, "to stand on guard against any move to revive this concept.…" In other words, Pearson was to be alert to any attempt by Imperial Britain to co-opt Canada.

The High Commissioner was Vincent Massey, whom King appointed to London in late 1935. Pearson found Massey formal, reserved, and awkward. He wasn't comfort-able greeting tourists or sports teams, Pearson observed. Pearson was more generous than Hume Wrong, who found Massey lazy, effete, and patronizing when he had worked for him in Washington. Later, Massey was said to be anti-Semitic too. The difference between Wrong and Pearson was restraint. Whether Pearson disliked Massey, he kept quiet. He knew that Massey was a patron who had given help in the past and could still. As Pearson told a farewell dinner hosted by Canada House in London in 1941, he had often been the beneficiary of his and Massey's intertwined for-tunes. He knew that Massey had been instrumental in get-ting him to Oxford and had promoted him in London. Massey was still on his way up. Pearson was on his way up too, and he knew to be nice without being insincere. Canada House was a small but distinguished mission, and those who worked there in the late 1930s would go very high indeed. A photograph taken in 1936 shows Massey, Pearson, and Vanier in full diplomatic dress—two future Governors General and a future prime minister.

Pearson loved Britain but knew the difference between affection and affectation. He refused to go native as Massey and others had done. He loved dining at the Traveller's Club on Pall Mall, wearing his black homburg, short black coat, and striped trousers, carrying a furled umbrella. "Anyone watching me … might have thought I was the patterned product of Eton, Oxford, and the Foreign Office, unless he heard me speak," he recalled. "I still talked Canadian. I had enough sense not to follow the unseemly example of some adult Canadians whom I watched as they tried to switch to English." This was not just a matter of style; it was the man himself, comfortable in his own skin. His reluctance to adopt all things English, however plummy, lovely, and brilliant, was a measure of his independence. "Mike was always an extremely good Canadian, a Canadian first, as well as an internationalist," said Malcolm MacDonald, the son of Ramsay MacDonald, Britain's prime minister in the 1930s. "He wasn't one of the old school. Mike … never wanted Britain to interfere as in old colonial times with Canada's right to make its own decision in international policy as well as national policy." Pearson had rejected airs at Oxford and he rejected them in London; he certainly never aspired to be a lord. Pearson was well-known around Buckingham Palace, but he said that if he were to call "Lords by their first names when I came back to Ottawa I was finished," suggesting little tolerance at home for poseurs. Much as he revelled in the social whirl and the company of those of rank and title, he never succumbed to their blandishments. On occasion, Pearson could play the "Canadian primitive," untutored in how to wear a gold-braided coat, but it was largely a put-on.

Indeed, he was amused by all the pomp and circumstance. He became part of ancient custom when he was appointed "Gold Stick in Waiting," or usher, at the coronation of George VI in 1937. If that meant rushing down to Moss Brothers to rent a costume of unknown origin—cocked hat, knee breeches, cutaway coat, and a sword—he treated it as a lark. If it meant pointless dress rehearsals and bowing and scraping at Westminster Abbey, it was all good fun.

He didn't take things of this kind too seriously, nor himself. This was the nature of the man. He knew that appeasing Canadian lumber lords angry that Russian timber was being used to build the viewing stand outside Canada House ("a real crisis," Pearson guffawed) was his responsibility too. The unfinished stand was torn down and rebuilt. "The honour of Canada was saved," he wrote. "Communist contamination was avoided." Pearson's moderation helped when he learned that King George would reverse the precedent set by his brother and no longer buy a Canadian car. "It will be a long time before certain people in this country realize that the King is the King of more than one country," Pearson told his diary.

THERE WAS MORE TO LIFE in London than gold sticks, foreign timber, and kings and cars. Pearson attended conferences on sugar and whaling and tried not to confuse the two, as he said. He loved London and liked diplomacy, but he was frustrated with Ottawa. When he was approached by the newly formed Canadian Broadcasting Corporation (CBC) to take a senior position in early 1937, he used the offer as leverage in advancing his public service career. The negotiations, which historian J.L. Granatstein carefully reconstructs in *The Ottawa Men*, lasted more than a year. Pearson said he didn't want to play one organization against the other, but he did just that. He wanted a promotion and more money (the CBC was offering $6,000, which was more than he was getting) and he let his masters know. While the department wouldn't have regretted losing Hume Wrong, Pearson's stock had risen. Skelton now praised Pearson's congeniality and judgment. The loose-jointed attic-dweller "would be a great calamity to lose.… We are all both proud and very fond of him." External Affairs promoted Pearson and gave him a good raise. Here again, Pearson was wilier than he let on. He cared about his career and he cared about money, though not obsessively. When opportunities arose, he either took them or used them to enhance his position.

Pearson wasn't shy. To earn money, he began making radio broadcasts for the shortwave service of the BBC in 1936. He used a pseudonym, Michael Macdonald, and disguised his voice. In one broadcast, on November 11, 1937, he reflected on the Great War, which had ended nineteen years earlier. During the customary two minutes of silence that brought London to a halt on that morning, he told his listeners that he was reminded of his war, "trudging in the mud; the sound of a bugle at camp at nightfall; the rusty old squadron gramophone. Friends who never saw Canada again—but who'll never see old age, distress or disillusionment either.…"

Pearson watched the march to the next war with anxiety, but he embraced neither the interventionism of Churchill nor the appeasement of Chamberlain. By the Imperial Conference in May 1937, at which Pearson lamented that King typically did nothing that would commit Canada to a common defence policy, he was not sure where Hitler was taking Germany. He knew that the Germans were rearming and that they had reoccupied the Rhineland, flouting the Versailles Treaty. But that didn't bother him. In fact, he agreed with *The Times* (London) that expelling Germany was "war-mongering." As he later wrote, "I was not yet fully aware of the menacing implications of Nazi policies." Pearson's view then was close to that of his masters, Skelton and King. Both were devout isolationists who opposed intervention until war was declared. (Another isolationist was Escott Reid, who would join the department in 1938 and later on become one of its most impassioned internationalists.)

Most important, Pearson's views up to 1938 were also close to those of Vincent Massey, who believed in Neville Chamberlain and appeasement. Then they began to diverge, and Charles Ritchie noted the difference between the two Canadians: "Mr. Massey was 100 percent Chamberlain and Mike wasn't. Mike was a very realistic friend of Britain and the British, very Canadian, very unlikely to be taken in by the charms of the social life which the British in those days were very good at laying on and to which Mr. Massey was rather susceptible...." He certainly was. Massey was a British Canadian. He was friends with the royal family and moved with the Cliveden Set, an influential clique of politicians and plutocrats who gathered at the country home of the Astors in Buckinghamshire outside London. His friends and associates, quite naturally, were wealthy patricians, usually Conservatives. Some were unfazed by Hitler; some were sympathetic to the Nazis. And some were anti-Semites.

Of course, there was another side, articulated by Winston Churchill and "the troublesome young men" around him who saw what was coming. But Pearson was unpersuaded. He didn't doubt Hitler until later. When it came to seeing the horrors in Germany in the second half of the decade, there was only a whisper of what economist Barbara Ward would memorably call, in another context, "that shrewd yet visionary voice." Pearson's memoirs scarcely mention Hitler's war upon on the Jews, which was well in train by 1937, or the atrocities of the Spanish Civil War. Pearson was wise and perceptive in many things, but not here. In his response to the Nazis—in private or public—he was slow, late, and tepid.

In March 1937, he heard the anti-appeasement argument directly from its greatest champion. It was at a small dinner at Claridge's in London. The guest speaker was Winston Churchill, who was in the depths of his political exile; he was in Parliament and in the press, but out of power and out of favour. He compared the military strength of Germany with that of France and Britain and predicted war within the year. He thought the Germans would vanquish the French quickly. Churchill's words seemed to have a modest impact on Pearson, who wanted to believe that war could be avoided.

When the Nazis annexed Austria in March 1938, Pearson's isolationism began to crack. "No longer was it possible for me to believe that Nazism was a temporary aberration in German politics, that the good sense of the German people would soon take care of the Fuhrer," he wrote. His remaining doubts were erased when Hitler made his claim on the Sudetenland in Czechoslovakia that summer. Pearson knew that war was coming, and he felt that collective security was a necessity. When Neville Chamberlain made his broadcast to the nation on September 27, Britons were digging trenches and Pearson's children were packing suitcases (they were to go to boarding school in Canada). The family was weeping. When Chamberlain returned from Munich waving that piece of paper promising peace, there was widespread relief that war had been avoided. But Pearson thought it had only been postponed.

Practically speaking, he could not quarrel with Britain's decision not to fight. He believed that the time bought by the Munich Agreement—time that was used to rearm the British military—may have saved the country from defeat later. (Another argument is that a strong show of force would have forced Hitler to back down, as it would have when he seized the Rhineland in 1936.) With his thinking evolving, Pearson now considered isolationism morally unacceptable. He wrote Skelton in 1939: "If I am tempted to become cynical and isolationist, I think of Hitler screeching into the microphone, Jewish women and children in ditches on the Polish border, Göring, the genial ape-man, and Goebbels, the evil imp, and then, whatever the British side may represent, the other does indeed stand for savagery and barbarism." He thought it may be true, as Massey insisted, that there are "seventy-five million decent Germans who love peace," but Pearson wasn't persuaded. In March 1939, when Hitler swallowed the rest of Czechoslovakia, he knew it was just a matter of time.

BEYOND BUSINESS, there was family. Mike and Maryon, children in tow, climbed into their Chevrolet and roamed England from Land's End to John o'Groats and loved it. Geoffrey, now twelve, accompanied his father to the soccer matches at Wembly to watch Arsenal. He and his sister, Patricia, now ten, watched the coronation parade of

George VI from their father's window at Canada House on Trafalgar Square. They spent summers near the ocean in Brittany and Wales and learned to ski in Switzerland. Geoffrey said that his four years in England taught him "to rely on my inner self," without close friends, learning to show a stiff upper lip. Whatever his adjustment, this was by all accounts a wonderful time in their lives. "We became established and comfortable, and were a happy family," said Mike.

On June 30, 1939, Mike, Maryon, and the children returned to Canada for the summer on their home leave. Pearson had a sense of foreboding that not even the warmth of the extended family gathering at Lac du Bonnet in Manitoba could dissolve. When he paddled to the post office in August and saw an ominous newspaper headline ("Nazis threaten Danzig and the Polish Corridor"), he knew he had to get back to London. He left immediately for Ottawa, where he boldly asked Skelton whether he could fly to London on the Pan American Super Clipper, which had just begun service from New York. Flying was rare in those days, but Skelton reluctantly agreed.

Pearson met King at his summer home in Kingsmere, in the Gatineau Hills. The prime minister couldn't understand why he was cutting short his leave. With the same kind of horrifying naïveté that persuaded him that Hitler was "Joan of Arc" and "Churchill was one of the most dangerous men I have ever known," King saw no war—even as the armies were mobilizing. But Pearson understood that as soon as the Germans and Soviets signed their non-aggression pact on August 23, Hitler had a free hand to invade Poland, which he did on September 1. Britain declared war on Germany on September 3. Canada followed on September 10. The great cataclysm had begun. The declaration of war affected veterans of the Great War particularly. Pearson lamented: "To those of us who remembered 5 August 1914 and the awful years that followed, this all seemed incredible. Before we had forgotten the dead of one war, our sons were to be killed in another. How could man be so mad?"

CHAPTER FOUR

Pearson's War

Finally, the much-feared war was on. And once again, as he was for other epochal events of the century, Mike Pearson would be at the centre of things. He would spend this war not as a combatant, but as a diplomat in different posts. He would ride the crest of events from London to Ottawa to Washington. He had a way of being where the action was—and this brought him opportunity. The war would deepen Pearson's commitment to a Canada that had the independence to act in the world, and to a system of collective international security. Here his nationalism and internationalism marched in lockstep. In London, where the Phony War of the fall of 1939 and the winter of 1940 gave way to real war in the spring, Pearson found himself caught up in a life that was "active, exciting and purposeful." Beyond the consular work of helping Canadians in distress, Pearson was in charge of coordinating the war effort between Britain, a country under siege, and Canada, its loyal dominion. But there was a big difference between now and 1914: Canada was at war because it wanted to be, not because it had to be. Not that the British always saw it that way. To the old imperialists in London, Canada was still a member of the Empire, which should stand "ready, aye, ready."

Much of Pearson's work in London consisted—as it would in Washington, in a different way—of petitioning a government to understand the desire of—and the necessity for—Canada to make its own decisions. In matters military, it was resisting the blithe British impulse to see Canada's forces as a part of Britain's, under their direction. As Pearson said, Canada's unalterable position was to control its overseas forces and "maintain their separate Canadian identity." It was a challenge to bring Canadian forces overseas "into line with our position as a fully self-governing state," so this assertion had to be made again and again in the early days of the war. "It took time, patience, and firmness to change the colonial mentality which lingered in certain quarters in Whitehall," he recalled. Unlike in 1914, Canada was no longer ready to supply men and material to form part of the British Imperial forces.

If Pearson wasn't sparring with London, he was sparring with Ottawa. Now that Canada was in the war, he wanted it to fight fully. Ottawa did not. King had resisted any policy (as he had the sanctions at the League of Nations) that might provoke a war that he had denied would ever happen. Now, with the war on, he resisted a commitment to win it. Pearson said that the British saw the conflict as a life-and-death struggle, but not Canada. When it came to negotiating the Commonwealth Air Training Program in 1939, for example, the British hoped to train twenty thousand pilots at fifty-two airfields in Canada. Pearson imagined "a stupendous program which will stagger them in Ottawa." But he knew that this commitment would require vigour, ambition, and "100 per cent enthusiasm for the war," which he doubted existed. To his diary, Pearson complained about Ottawa's lethargy. The commitment was diluted; it would be "many pilots a year" rather than the hoped-for twenty thousand. "Some apparently still think there that a war can be conducted in second gear," he moaned. Eventually, though, fifty thousand or more pilots were trained and Franklin D. Roosevelt would call Canada "the aerodrome of democracy," words that Pearson wrote for him.

Pearson's continuing problem was serving the whims and wishes of a difficult master. He understood the timid, mercurial prime minister, and he knew he was hard to please. In Pearson's memoir, written long after King was gone, his tone is always careful and cordial, if a touch impatient; it conveys less of the respect he had for R.B. Bennett and none of the affection he had for Louis St. Laurent. In his diary, which Pearson kept for ten years before and after his time in London, he complains of King's vanity, *amour propre*, and stupidity. But Pearson maintained good relations, even though managing an egotistical man wasn't easy. When the self-important prime minister sent windy, trivial, multi-page encrypted telegrams to Whitehall that took hours for over-whelmed British ciphers to decode, it was Pearson who had to tell Ottawa, gently, that in future a one-page, uncoded message would suffice. If the eccentric prime minister cabled ("secrete and most immediate") the High Commission requesting stones from Westminster Hall, which had been damaged in an air raid the night before, it was Pearson who dutifully arranged to gather, crate, and ship them to Canada so King could put them among his ruins at Kingsmere, where they stand today. The greatest test of Pearson's diplo-macy was less how he managed the British than how he mol-lified the Canadians.

By 1940, events were cascading upon each other. The fall of France. The ascent of Winston Churchill. The evacuation from Dunkirk. The Battle of Britain. The London Blitz. In the mysterious arc of life, the son of a reverend born in a hamlet across the ocean found himself witness to history's great conflagration. Mike approached it with wryness. One

Sunday afternoon during the Battle of Britain, which he called "the greatest air battle of all time," he played a round of golf outside London. His caddy advised him to slice to the right, as there was a time bomb buried on the left of the fairway. Later in their game, they discovered a bomb crater on the eleventh tee. His great worry was concentrating on his game amid the hazards and the din of bombs and the anti-aircraft fire. "We had a lot of fun," he wrote home. "Every time I heard any signs of aerial activity I would put on my tin helmet ... not so much as protection against falling shrapnel as to improve my score by forcing me to keep my head down."

Pearson loved the drama. When the fleet of smacks, trawlers, and sailboats crossed the Channel at Dunkirk to bring home the Tommies trapped on the beaches, he and Charles Ritchie drove down from London to watch. The island was about to be invaded and Pearson said that if the British were to surrender like the French, Canada should cut its ties and become a republic. Among the Canadians, the French were in bad odour. In a letter to Maryon, one of the few of this period to survive, Pearson describes Alice Massey, the wife of the High Commissioner, attacking the French in the presence of Pauline Vanier, the wife of Canada's chargé d'affaires in Paris. Madame Vanier had just fled France under fire. Mrs. Massey asked her: "When you are safely back in Canada, will you think of us being bombed to pieces over here [*sic*]." Pearson wrote to Maryon that he "felt like strangling her." Mrs. Massey could be as insufferable as her husband.

As for wives, there was a tempest when Pearson, Hume Wrong, and George Crerar, the military attaché, implored their wives to join their children in Canada in June 1940. (Maryon had rejoined Mike after his abrupt return to London in 1939.) None of the women wanted to go home, but after much argument, all acquiesced. Once on the boat in Southampton though, Joyce Wrong slipped off and retrieved her baggage. When Maryon learned of this, she felt terribly betrayed.

For the next six months, the bombs fell constantly. One night in October, the roof of the apartment house next to Pearson's was aflame. When he and others rushed to help put out the fire, a stern sergeant major barred their way and warned: "Tenants, sir, are not permitted on the roof." When Pearson protested, he said firmly, "I'm afraid it is the rule, sir. I'll deal with the fire." Which he did.

Pearson was without Maryon in London, but he wasn't alone. With him in Canada House was a luminous supporting cast only Canada could have assembled: Hume Wrong, the imperious polymath; George Ignatieff, the aristocratic

Russian émigré; and Charles Ritchie, the amorous aesthete whose lifetime of adventures in love and statecraft would fill four volumes of elegant diaries. Despite the anxiety of invasion and nocturnal diversion, they were a happy band.

ON JANUARY 28, 1941, O.D. Skelton collapsed and died. His death was a blow to the young service, for which he had been midwife, governess, and tutor. Although Pearson had complained privately of Skelton's administrative lassitude, he appreciated Skelton's extraordinary talent. Within an hour, King named Norman Robertson acting undersecretary. This surprised and hurt Pearson; Robertson was six years younger and had joined the service the year after Pearson, at a lower level. Pearson thought the job should be his (as did Hume Wrong) and let King know. Pearson later called it the biggest professional disappointment of his life. But when Robertson's appointment was made permanent, Pearson accepted it gracefully. Months later, knowing that tongues were wagging in the wartime capital, he praised Robertson in a speech in Ottawa shortly after his return from London. Historian Adam Chapnick claims that he made the speech "with reluctance" and that he was "jealous" of Robertson. If there was tension, it didn't last. "Among Mike's many fine qualities was his complete lack of anything that could be called jealousy," recalled Max Wershof, a junior officer, his view echoed by others. This didn't mean that Pearson wasn't offended when Robertson lamely suggested later on that he serve in Brazil, which was far from international events.

Pearson returned to Ottawa in June 1941. On leaving London, he paid public tribute to the besieged British at a farewell banquet: "God knows those people are not perfect. They have defects enough. At times their methods seem to me to be based on Plantagenet ideas, applied with Victorian ease. They often make me tear my hair. But, by and large, I feel that this county represents the furthest and finest stage mankind has yet reached in political and social development." He was pleased, he said, to be a Canadian, with a line of national development stretching "from the Magna Carta to the Sirois Commission." From those roots, he said, came great branches.

PEARSON'S SOJOURN IN OTTAWA was brief. Although he was happy to be reunited with his family, he was unhappy about being home. He bargained for a defined position and more money—and got both. He was now assistant undersecretary to Robertson. In 1942, a year or so after he had returned to Canada, he was sent to Washington as minister-counsellor. Leighton McCarthy, the Toronto lawyer whom

King had appointed to replace Loring Christie as minister to the United States (there was no ambassador at that time), disliked Hume Wrong, his deputy; he wanted Pearson instead. Robertson was "rather broken up at having to give up Pearson," King wrote in his diary that May.

Pearson didn't ask to go to Washington; in fact, he fretted about the big house at 301 Buena Vista Road that he'd bought in Rockcliffe and about uprooting his family again, but he couldn't refuse. His new assignment would put him in the seat of the world's rising power. The centre of gravity had shifted to the United States when it entered the war after Japan attacked Pearl Harbor on December 7, 1941. Although Britain had not lost the war when it stood alone for those two years, it had not won it either. And could not, not on its own. Only the intervention of the United States would turn the tide (as well as the might and blood of Soviet Russia, which Hitler had invaded on June 22, 1941). Once again, managing Canada's role would take agility and delicacy. Once again, this task would fall to Mike Pearson.

When he arrived in the oppressive Washington summer, the capital was in a frenzy. America was expanding its military and retooling its economy. It was feverishly throwing up a wartime bureaucracy; the Pentagon, the world's largest office building, would arise in sixteen months. When Hitler declared war on the United States, he underestimated not only its willingness to fight but also its ability to improvise. To Washington, Pearson brought mixed views about the relationship between the United States and Canada. "Are you an American?" he asked rhetorically in a lecture he gave in Britain in 1941. "Yes, I am a Canadian," he answered shrewdly, understanding perfectly how the colossus had insinuated itself into the Canadian psyche. He was not as fond of America as of Britain, for which he had a deep sentimentality. He had been much relieved to come home from Chicago in 1921; in the early 1940s, he still found the Americans aggressive and crude, and it would take him time to learn to appreciate them. At a party celebrating Franklin Roosevelt's birthday on January 30, 1943, Pearson recoiled at the gaudiness of Hollywood celebrity at the Mayflower Hotel ("noisy, crowded affair, juvenile and boisterous") and winced when Lord Halifax was lampooned. Pearson liked the Lord, forgiving his outspoken enthusiasm for appeasement and for accommodating the Nazis in 1940, and the affair offended him. In behaviour and decorum, Pearson always had standards.

Naturally, Pearson made friends in Washington. They included James "Scotty" Reston of *The New York Times* and Dean Acheson, a senior official of the State Department who would become its secretary. Acheson knew Canada; he was the son of Eleanor Gertrude Gooderham, of the prominent Canadian family of distillers and bankers. As a student, he had spent a summer laying track around Hudson Bay.

Pearson identified Acheson early as a comer in Washington and courted him. They had a warm relationship, and there was also much laughter and conviviality between them and their wives. They had uproarious times. Once, at Pearson's rented cottage in Chevy Chase, Maryland, they were on the screened porch in a heavy summer thunderstorm. "Let's take to the boats, take to the boats!" cried one of the guests. Soon the inebriated party was up on the dining table, pretending to row furiously, accepting some swimmers and refusing others in an alcohol-inspired system of triage. Pearson would become known in other circles too. He appeared on a radio quiz show and organized baseball games on Sundays between Canadians and members of the State Department. For refreshment, they would set up a pitcher of martinis at first base, requiring all those who reached it to down one, ensuring no team overwhelmed the other.

If Anglo-Canadian relations were largely about fulfilling an obligation, American-Canadian relations were about avoiding absorption. Journalist Peter Stursberg notes that in

Britain, the Canadians were consulted whereas in Washington, they were ignored. Pearson worried that Canada was being treated as a subordinate to be ordered to do things rather than an ally to be asked. He frowned when the Americans, unfamiliar with Canada's struggle for status under the British, saw Canada as another state of the Union. Decisions were made and Canada was informed afterward, as part of "the British Empire." Once, the Big Two even decided to meet in Canada without bothering to tell Ottawa. From the American perspective, though, this indifference wasn't hard to understand. America, not Canada, was now Britain's biggest ally. From Canada's perspective, this demotion was humiliating. By 1942, Canada had been fighting for more than two years, and its contribution of men and material was relatively greater than America's. It was mostly Canadian soldiers who had died in the ill-fated raid on Dieppe, including Norman Young, Pearson's brother-in-law. Canada was training pilots. It was escorting, or would escort, half the convoys across the Atlantic. Its bombers would take a regular turn over Germany. At home, its mills, mines, and forests were fuelling the Allied war machine.

Predictably (if politely) Canada sought representation on the munitions and supply boards and on other committees, as well as more general recognition for its effort. It wanted authority, not just acknowledgment—something more than a pat on the head. Many of these concerns, big and small, occupied Pearson in Washington. Canada was so isolated that he had to "ferret out information" on civilian and military affairs with vulpine intensity.

Pearson also had to monitor every aspect of its various relationships to ensure Canada was part of the decision making. Would Canada have its own military mission in Washington, rather than a joint one with the British? (No, but Major General Maurice Pope headed a joint staff.) Would Canada be included in the announcement of the Allied landings at Sicily in 1943? (Yes, but only after Pearson made a personal plea to FDR.) Would Churchill invite Mackenzie King to join him on a visit to Washington if Churchill couldn't come to Ottawa? (Yes, but only after FDR issued an invitation too.) Did Canada have a seat at the table? Was it recognized here and there? The problem wasn't necessarily being squeezed between Britain and America either, as had been feared, it was being squeezed out entirely. As Pearson said in 1941, when the United States wanted Canada to kick the Free French off the islands of St. Pierre and Miquelon, "we were no banana republic to be pushed around by Washington." But the Americans didn't care about Canada's identity crisis. "If the British sometimes forgot the Statute of Westminster, the Americans hardly knew that it existed," Pearson recalled.

In response—perhaps as a defensive measure—Canada adopted the principle of "functionalism." Practically speaking, this meant that Canada sought representation and responsibility for decisions only where, as Pearson said, Canada "had a very real and direct interest in the work and could make an important contribution to it." Ultimately, this measured approach brought some acts of recognition, but not as many as Pearson had hoped. Once again he felt let down by Ottawa, particularly by the unassertive Mackenzie King.

When it came to the war, King was content to be seen—but not heard—with the Big Two. At the Anglo-American conferences in Quebec City in 1943 and 1944, King wasn't in the room for the talks but was sure to appear afterward for the joint photographs. He was a prop, a happy accessory, between Roosevelt and Churchill. King believed that acting as an occasional intermediary between these two titans, if that was how he saw himself, was more useful than being a silent bystander in their negotiations. In 1998, the government of Quebec underscored his absence at the table when it erected a statue honouring Churchill and FDR but not King. The reality was that King should have represented

Canada, as Pearson and others knew. By 1945, Canada was fielding the world's fourth largest military. Its soldiers had landed on Juno Beach at Normandy and had liberated much of Holland. Yet recognition was a struggle both because of King's reticence and Churchill's and Roosevelt's indifference.

WHILE MUCH OF HIS TIME was still spent managing the changing bilateral relationship, Pearson started to contemplate the challenges of a postwar world. Pearson began taking part in multilateral discussions on international bodies after his arrival as minister in 1942. His herculean efforts continued after he became ambassador to the United States on January 1, 1945 (the mission had become an embassy the year before) and continued until his departure in October 1946. Pearson was hardly new to international conferences, but he now became a leading player. His work in Washington to help establish the early architecture of the postwar era propelled him to prominence. It was the making of a statesman.

Pearson's imagination and energy brought these important international bodies to life. His work began as representative to the United Nations Relief and Rehabilitation Administration (UNRRA), which Ottawa had agreed to support in 1942. As an affluent country, Canada expected to be involved in the rebuilding of Europe. It also expected to be on the Central Policy Committee, where decisions were made. When the Russians and Americans refused, Pearson told them that if Canada did not have a say on the controlling body, it wouldn't sign the convention. A compromise allowed Canada to chair the Supply Committee and attend sessions of the Policy Committee. This gave Pearson a seat at the table. The commitment took up almost half his time between 1943 and 1946, and sent him to Berlin, Poland, and back to Geneva. He'd spent much time at the League of Nations before the war. There he was greeted by a familiar porter at the Hotel de la Paix after an absence of ten years and asked if he wanted his old room. He found his visit to the ruins of eastern Europe particularly disturbing.

The body in which Pearson played an especially critical role was the Food and Agriculture Organization (FAO). When the founding conference was held at the baronial resort hotel in Hot Springs, West Virginia, in May 1943, Pearson was one of five representatives from Canada among several hundred from many other countries. Soon he was on the Steering Committee. In Washington, in July, he was elected chairman of its Interim Commission. He accepted though it meant cancelling his summer holidays. Workaholic that he was, he didn't flinch. His contribution was pivotal; he mediated between sides and drafted the charter constitution. When the FAO was formally established in Quebec in October 1945—the first of the agencies of the United Nations—the organization wanted him to become its first director general. Pearson declined. He didn't want to leave the foreign service now, and even if he had, he knew agriculture was not his métier. But the success of his chairmanship of the FAO Interim Commission and the prospect of candidacy for director general reflected his growing international stature. By the mid-1940s, Pearson was the best-known Canadian around, his fame rivalled only by Barbara Ann Scott, the figure skater. "You are becoming a very important person in the International world," enthused Georges P. Vanier in 1943. He was.

These were heady days. In addition to his work with the better-known organizations, Pearson was busy creating other instruments of postwar co-operation, such as the international aviation agency, and addressing other pressing questions, such as the uses of atomic energy. These talks often conveniently took place in Washington. Thus Canada's diplomat-in-chief found himself cruising the Potomac River on the presidential yacht with Harry Truman on November 11, 1945. Aware of the poignancy of discussing atomic power on Armistice Day, Pearson used the occasion to appeal to the president to urge the United Nations to control this awful new force. He advocated "internationalization." This opportunity to have real influence was all in a day's work for Pearson; it was the life he led. If Pearson's plea had a hint of moralism, it also had pragmatism. By 1944, there was much talk of a new international idealism, such as Wendell Willkie's "One World." Pearson wasn't a dreamer, and didn't think there could be one world, even though he was an internationalist—even a world federalist. He did, however, believe in collective security and the need for nations to cede sovereignty to a higher authority, though he knew this would not readily happen. As much as he was a romantic, he was a realist too. He had seen the League of Nations fail and he didn't want that to happen to the United Nations.

Bit by bit, Pearson was helping to assemble the pieces of the new world order—establishing humanitarian relief, addressing food and agricultural aid, curtailing atomic arms. In creating the United Nations itself, though, Pearson did not play a big role. It's often assumed that he was one of its framers because the United Nations eventually became his sandbox, the forum of many of his diplomatic triumphs. But Canada was not invited to the conference at Dumbarton Oaks in 1944 where the structure and aims of the new organization were established.

Pearson's contribution to the United Nations was limited to pushing for a greater role for middle powers among great powers. He also tried to persuade the Americans to embrace an international body that would limit their independence, as it would all members. Pearson was foreshadowing one of the important roles he would play there, as a moderator of American power. At the conference in San Francisco establishing the United Nations in 1945, Canada was eclipsed by Australia, and Pearson was eclipsed by Norman Robertson and Hume Wrong, who had larger roles. But when it came time to choose the United Nations' first Secretary-General, it was Pearson, not Wrong or Robertson, whom the West wanted. But for the Soviets, the job would have been his. Wrong said that Pearson had dodged a bullet, that running the United Nations would have been endlessly frustrating. When the Soviets exercised their veto over his nomination again in 1953, Pearson said dolefully that it was "the only job I ever wanted."

The war was over and things were changing at home. In 1946, Louis St. Laurent had been appointed secretary of state for external affairs, the first representative of the department in cabinet. He asked Pearson to become his undersecretary. Pearson was not enamoured of the idea; he wanted to stay in Washington or go to London as High Commissioner.

Then again, this was the top job. It was the post he had been denied five years earlier, and many immediately saw it as a prelude to the most extraordinary chapter in the accelerating life of Lester Pearson. Of course, it was.

CHAPTER FIVE

Canada's Boy Wonder

In the spring of 1947, the year after Mike Pearson returned from his glorious American summer, he turned fifty. There is no suggestion that he suffered a mid-life crisis—if such an identifiable state of mind existed before the pop culture era—or had any doubt about his progress at a half-century. Then again, his life was full. While he always insisted he had no grand design—no consuming desire to build skyscrapers, cure cancer, or become prime minister—things were unfolding purposefully.

By any measure, his two score and ten were successful. He had gone to war and survived it, he had tried business and left it, he had studied at Oxford and loved it, he had taught history and lived it. He had married and raised two adoring children to adulthood. Unlike other extraordinary lives, he always had choices, and each time he chose wisely. Connections helped. Judgment and timing did too. In 1928, he wisely traded a seat in the Ivy Tower for one by the Peace Tower; later on, instead of serving in Japan in the 1930s or

Brazil in the 1940s, he went to London and Washington as the locus of power shifted from the old world to the new. At just the right moment, he had joined a legion of Renaissance men who believed that Canada could make a difference in the world, recognizing, as Shakespeare put it, that "tide in the affairs of men, which taken at the flood, leads on to fortune." Surely it did for him. Pearson rose in the Department of External Affairs until he came to run it. In his memoir, he explained that he had advanced without outside influence or wealth: "I had done it by hard work and long hours, by making it evident that I was available for whatever was to be done; by welcoming every opportunity for new and more responsible duties; and by accumulating all the experience possible in all the varied aspects of my profession." Now, after nineteen years of late nights and lost summers, the first secretary was undersecretary. He was the High Priest. Lord knows, he'd earned it.

He had become the indispensable man in that travelling carnival of conclaves of the 1940s. When the Allies began planning the peace, he was the face of Canada, recognized and applauded everywhere. A profile in *Maclean's* in 1944 typified the adoring press notices, cooing that Pearson had "a finely-trained mind, a solid-built rock-ribbed physique ... and almost boundless energy" making him, as a diplomat, "one of Canada's very best." He was disarming, funny, boy-ish, a regular guy who chopped wood, played tennis, and defiantly wore short sleeves among the stuffed shirts of the staid diplomatic world. It's hard to find a discouraging word about him in those days. Pearson liked reporters and they liked him. He was one of the most popular and accessible sources, happy to share selective information with journalists such as Bruce Hutchison, Grant Dexter, and Blair Fraser. "Maybe that's one of the reasons we like him—he trusts us," wrote Fraser in 1951. They returned the favour with valen-tines in pink envelopes marked "Dynamic Diplomat" and "Canada's 'Boy Wonder.'"

Not all of the press got it right, but who cared? Readers could learn how Pearson became "Mike" because he looked like a cartoon Irishman, that he went to Oxford on a Rhodes Scholarship, that he chose diplomacy because politics, his first choice, was dull and provincial. In one fanciful account in a foreign-language publication, Pearson is called the son of a "physicist," summoned to his nation's service by the celestial appearance of "Mackenzie" outside his door. As the story goes, "Mackenzie" begs him to join his govern-ment. Pearson agrees. This fable would have amused the self-deprecating Pearson if he ever saw it. Anyway, a little hyperbole never hurt anyone, least of all Mike Pearson, who was now levitating through life.

Whenever Pearson's work was celebrated in these years—that glorious season from the early 1940s until the late 1950s called "the golden age of Canadian diplomacy"—Canada was celebrated too. He was representing a country that had broken with the isolationism of the 1920s and 1930s and embraced a spirited internationalism. This was no small thing for a thinly populated, parochial nation with a colonial mentality. For Canadians, it was a dramatic new way of seeing themselves beyond their shores.

At fifty, who was Mike Pearson? He was five feet, ten inches, about 165 pounds. His frame was taut yet supple, retaining the fitness of an athlete well into middle age. (In his early forties, he beat a Canadian tennis champion, Georges LeClair, in two sets.) After almost two decades of cocktails and canapés, Pearson had neither the jowls, paunch, nor pallor of the diplomat. In fact, he remained youthful, often described as a "golden boy" until he was sixty. His facial features were distinctive and mobile. His smile was easy and impish. A shock of auburn hair often hung over his forehead, barely hiding a receding hairline. In dress, he favoured double-breasted suits and polka-dot bow ties (which were deemed too professorial when he became opposition leader), although in essence "he didn't really care what he wore," said his son, Geoffrey.

Among the fund of adjectives used to describe him— "cherubic," "informal," "charming," "energetic"—a favourite was "rumpled." He had stamina, which is why, when necessary, he could get by on as little as two hours' sleep. His pleasures were playing golf and tennis and, later, watching hockey or baseball on television. There was also reading, usually biography or history. He had little interest in food, although he loathed salads and loved pie. Things mechanical exasperated him. He owned paintings (David Milnes, acquired at $25 apiece in the 1940s) but little else of value. As prime minister, he initially drove a humble Rambler; when the brakes disengaged at Harrington Lake, it rolled down the hill and crashed. His homes were modest and he complained that he lost money buying and selling them. Although he was called an elitist, he protested that "my tastes aren't very high," as his unpretentious basement study suggests. His manner was disarming and mild. Geoffrey never heard him swear; "damn" seemed to be the most emphatic, and he would apologize for his indiscretion. He never raised his voice and seldom became angry. He was able to see both sides of an argument, often to his detriment. He rarely felt despair, likely because there was little for him to despair about; his life was without illness, divorce, debt, or major disappointment. He wasn't close to his brothers, one of whom, Vaughan, never recovered psychologically from the Great War. While he made friends easily ("You meet Mike Pearson two or three times and you begin to think of him as an old pal," recalled Blair Fraser), there were few intimates. "I think it is fair to say that he was my closest friend, but I cannot speak for him," said Walter Gordon in the 1970s. Gordon had organized Pearson's leadership campaign, assured his financial security, and served in his cabinet. "I doubt if he thought I was his closest friend. I just don't know."

Family mattered most. Pearson's long absences and long hours were a strain that all bore cheerfully. One of the more aching memories of this separation is Pearson's recollection of a scratchy two-minute telephone call he placed on Christmas 1940, from London to his family in Winnipeg, a war and an ocean between them. By 1947, his children had grown up. They had been raised by nannies and rarely saw their father. Yet both loved him deeply. Pearson worried whether he was as good to them as his father had been to him ("I am acutely conscious of my own failures as a father," he confessed in 1951), but they gave him no reason. Patsy was eighteen. She went to university and eventually married a doctor. Geoffrey was twenty. After a succession of boarding schools, he was at the University of Toronto. Like his father, he would go to Oxford and join the foreign service. Over the years Pearson came to trust his son's judgment more than most knew. After his father's death, Geoffrey dutifully organized his papers, eulogized his diplomacy in an insightful book, and became the chief custodian of his memory.

In 1947, Mike and Maryon had been married twenty-two years. Their marriage wasn't perfect. Maryon spared no one her withering judgments. Patsy said her mother had little time for her. "There was no praise," she told Heather Robertson in *More Than a Rose* in 1991. "In letters, yes, but not to your face. She was a very, very critical person. I felt constrained at home. I was always backing away from her. She could cut you off at the knees. I was intimidated by my mother." Maryon could, and did, pack the children off to relatives or boarding school; in a diary she kept when she accompanied Mike to the London Naval Conference in 1930, she scarcely mentions the two infants she left behind. Her daughter-in-law, Landon, who would have five children, become a champion of children's rights, and serve ably in the Senate of Canada, was always reluctant to tell Maryon when she was pregnant: "She thought there was something vaguely obscene about it."

Maryon's distemper produced memorable bon mots. She was the smartest of the prime ministerial wives, as columnist Charles Lynch said, and she was also the sauciest. The euphemism of choice for Maryon was "tart." In public she could be snobbish, defensive, pugnacious, and aloof, wearing veils and dark glasses and throwing off cheeky remarks, a tableau of cranky, artless frankness. "Une dame formidable," sighed a Quebec MP. "She was her own worst enemy," says Landon Pearson. In 1964, when Maryon read a profile of herself written by the talented Christina McCall Newman of *Maclean's*, she telephoned her with a string of unhappy rejoinders. "You're just so *young*," she fumed. "Only someone as *young* as you are could be so indiscreet." Yet indiscretion never inhibited Maryon. "How does it feel to be back in the West?" she was once asked. "Not very good," she replied. If her bluntness disturbed Mike, he never let on. She wisely handled their money (including investing the $38,500 Pearson received with his Nobel Prize in 1957), managed twenty-two different homes during their marriage, and was always loyal. She campaigned with her husband in the lean years and called Diefenbaker "that awful man." Her advice was sometimes "very bad," an associate of her husband says, but generally "no worse than most."

In *Political Wives*, journalist Susan Riley calls the Pearsons' relationship "conventional, patriarchal." She twice suggests that this was because Maryon was "many years his junior." In fact, the difference was less than five years. As for conventional, not necessarily. In their younger days, Mike and Maryon were part of Ottawa's smart set. Both drank (she more heavily than he), both liked dancing (she much more than he), witty conversation, and gaiety. Both also enjoyed the attentions of the opposite sex. Maryon was close to Graham Towers, for twenty years the governor of the Bank of Canada. Handsome, wealthy, and elegant, Towers was austere and cool by day and flirtatious and bawdy (he was known for his off-colour jokes in mixed company) by night. His libido was notorious; by all accounts, Towers loved women. The Pearsons often joined Towers and his wife, Mollie, at their rambling home in Murray Bay, Quebec. Sometimes Maryon drove there alone with Towers, Heather Robertson wrote, or flew off with him to weekend parties in Toronto. Towers's careful biographer, Douglas Fullerton, dares not ask but cites an anonymous friend who says, boldly, that Towers liked "Saturday nights." So did Maryon.

If Pearson accepted his wife's risqué relationship with Towers, it may have been because he had a *liaison dangereuse* of his own. In London, during the war, he had met Mary

Greey and her sister, Elizabeth, who were from Toronto. They were flatmates of Alison Grant, a niece of Vincent Massey, who would later marry George Ignatieff. Alison's brother was George Grant, the philosopher, who was studying at Oxford as a Rhodes Scholar. Mike began to see Mary. Alison said of her: "When she looks limpidly through her blue eyes people go absolutely weak." John English calls Mary "a scintillating companion in the absence of his [Pearson's] family during the 'siren years.'" William Christian, George Grant's biographer, calls their relationship an affair. In September 1941, Grant wrote his mother (under the warning "*strictly confidential* [not to be mentioned to a soul]") of Mary's wrenching departure from London and "all the love and affection that had brought her home." Mary was returning to Canada to be with Pearson. "Mary will obviously turn more and more upon Mike," Grant wrote. "All I want to say is, to understand and try and help. If you have ever seen Mary and Mike together you would know how absolutely suited they are for each other and how each adores the other. They are both far too fine to ever let it interfere with his children and wife, but please try to understand it and make it a natural easy thing."

Grant was right; Pearson did not let the relationship interfere with his marriage. After less than a year in Ottawa, he went to Washington, where he remained until 1946. Mary Greey returned to Britain in 1945 and married the eminent historian Gerald Graham. Greey, now ninety-two and deaf, refuses to discuss these years; her daughter says that her mother says she regrets her conversations with historians. When Christian's biography of George Grant appeared in 1993, Greey wrote Christian "a nasty letter" criticizing his indiscretion. But the story of Pearson and Greey doesn't end with their romance; in 1965, when Pearson was prime minister, George Grant published his venerated polemic, *Lament for a Nation*, in which he excoriated the Liberals for selling out Canada. He'd revealed his hostility to Pearson a year earlier in a harsh review of *The Four Faces of Peace*, a collection of Pearson's speeches and statements. Grant wondered why the book was "allowed to be written," ridden as it was with clichés, platitudes, and "attenuated pronouncements." In diplomacy, he dismisses Pearson as "a good committee man," an attribute that he thinks doesn't produce a "profundity of political analysis or subtlety of literary style." Privately, he called Pearson "the ambitious little bureaucrat." Grant's hostility was as much personal as intellectual: Mike was no longer the "nice person" he knew in London who had offered to help Grant find work when he returned from England as a student. According to Christian, Grant felt that Pearson was "a cad" in his relationship with Mary. Grant was angry that he "had strung Mary along, and treated her inexecrably" after she returned to Canada.

Whatever their diversions, Mike and Maryon survived, parting only upon his death. He rhapsodizes about her in his memoir, and at its end, is "gratified that she is relieved and happy" that he was no longer prime minister. When he died, she was disconsolate. The void he left, she told a friend, was so large that she couldn't believe he was gone. She grew more demanding after Mike's death; even her son found visiting her difficult. Three years later, Towers died. Now both men in her life were gone, and it was too much for her. In a rare public comment in 1974, Maryon said of Mike: "I was lucky to share 47 years of my life with this great man. Once, many years ago, I was asked by a Press woman what I liked best about my husband—I said that he was never *boring*. She thought this was not much of a reply but I always envied the women who sat next to him at large formal dinners because I knew they would enjoy the occasion [emphasis hers]."

WELL BEFORE PEARSON came back to Canada in October 1946 to run the Department of External Affairs, there was talk that he would enter politics. Mackenzie King had raised the prospect with him during a carriage ride through the

Bois de Boulogne in Paris the summer before. King thought highly of Pearson ("very modest, unassuming. He is going to be valuable to Robertson," he told his diary in 1941) and imagined him as prime minister one day. Pearson wasn't interested. Serving in King's cabinet was impossible for him. It wasn't just that King was a fussbudget, self-absorbed, and excessively cautious; their views of the world were different. His adventurism worried King, who told his diary in 1948: "The truth is our country has no business trying to play a world role in the affairs of nations, the very location of some of which our people know little or nothing about. So far as External Affairs is concerned, they have been allowed to run far too much on Pearson's sole say-so, and Pearson himself [has been] moved far too much by the kind of influences that are brought to bear upon him. He is young, idealistic, etc. but has not responsibility."

One reason that Pearson agreed to leave Washington for Ottawa—he anticipated going on to London as High Commissioner, which would have taken his career in another direction—was that Louis St. Laurent was succeeding King at External Affairs. Pearson revered St. Laurent ("I have known no finer gentleman, or one who had a greater sense of public duty"). It meant, as his deputy, that Pearson was free to pursue a muscular foreign policy. He knew, even as

King balked at his rashness and dismissed his belief in "the parliament of man," that he could rely on the support of his minister. It was, as Pearson notes, a perfect relationship. Pearson offered St. Laurent loyalty; St. Laurent offered Pearson latitude.

So, in 1948, when Pearson wondered how the West would respond to Soviet aggression, he wasn't inhibited by King's conservatism. The Soviets had invaded Czechoslovakia in February, and Pearson doubted that the United Nations could respond. He saw the necessity of a new regional organization that would marshal the moral, economic, diplomatic, and military power of the West against communism. The first expression of this idea as government policy came in a speech by Louis St. Laurent on April 29. He told the House of Commons that "the organization of collective defence … is the most effective guarantee of peace." Without sacrificing "the universality of the United Nations," he proposed that the free nations of the world form their own association of collective defence, under Article 51 of the UN Charter. Creating such an organization, he said, would not be "a counsel of despair but a message of hope." Pearson had written the speech.

Whether Canada was the first nation to propose the North Atlantic alliance, as some suggest, or not, Pearson believed absolutely in the idea and pursued it vigorously. Yet he thought of NATO as a short-term solution—not a second United Nations—which would fade away as it became unnecessary. Of course, it didn't. At the same time, he was passionately committed to Article 2, which Canada proposed in order to make the organization an economic, social, and political alliance. Dean Acheson called this idea "typical Canadian moralizing." That NATO didn't become the Atlantic community that he had envisioned was a disappointment to Pearson. Yet NATO was a seminal achievement, and it owed much to Pearson, as well as to Escott Reid, Norman Robertson, and Hume Wrong. It was no surprise that Pearson was asked to be NATO's first Secretary-General. Although he declined, he felt that NATO was his greatest achievement in foreign affairs. "It was not the most exciting thing with which I was associated, nor the most dramatic," he told a friend. "It was not even the most *immediately* important thing. But in the long run I think it was the most important."

There would be challenges aplenty for Pearson in those stirring years. In the spring of 1947, for example, he watched as the United Nations agonized in a special session over the future of Palestine. The British were withdrawing, leaving the problem to the United Nations. As one of the newly elected non-permanent members of the Security Council, Canada was appointed to the special committee of the General Assembly to decide Palestine's fate. Ultimately, it sided with the majority, which proposed the partition of the territory into Jewish and Arab states, with an economic union and a demilitarized Jerusalem. Pearson proposed a four-nation working group, which eventually drafted the terms that produced the State of Israel on May 14, 1948. He was chosen to be its chair, Geoffrey Pearson says, because he was a civil servant, was seen as impartial, knew the United Nations, and because "they needed a chairman and he was available." But while he knew the land and its history, Pearson was not a committed Zionist. Contrary to what some suggest, he wasn't predisposed to a Jewish state. He was under more pressure from Jews than from Arabs, to be sure, but he was, as usual, a pragmatist. Pearson's work was seen as pivotal, even as it was discouraged by Mackenzie King, who complained to his diary: "He [Pearson] likes keeping Canada at the head of everything, in the forefront in connection with UN affairs." When Pearson embraced partition, he was denounced by the Arabs and called "Rabbi Pearson" by the Israelis. To his underlings at External Affairs, biographer John Beal notes, "he was 'King of the Jews' behind his back."

In the summer of 1948, Mackenzie King was succeeded by St. Laurent. This meant that Pearson would have to address the question King had put to him two years earlier: would he leave the civil service, where he had security, for elective office, which he could lose tomorrow? "I was now faced with the most difficult decision that I had ever had to make," Pearson recalled. Actually, it wasn't *that* difficult. He had risen as far as he could in the department and he knew that the real decisions were made by ministers, not public servants. Moreover, the personal risk was minimal. The party had promised to find him a safe seat, and the government was likely to be returned with a majority. In the unlikely event that the Liberals should win and Pearson should lose, St. Laurent could reappoint him to the public service, as King suggested he would. If all went according to plan, as it always did in those days in Liberal Canada, Pearson would follow the example of St. Laurent, who had been recruited by King in 1941, named minister of justice, and had then found a seat in Parliament.

Once again, the stars were aligned for Pearson. As minister, he would be running the department he knew inside out, he would be joining a majority government in the least partisan of portfolios, and he would have the confidence of the prime minister. And if it went terribly wrong for him at home, the supernova who had been courted for the top jobs at NATO and the United Nations would not be looking for work for long; in 1947, he had turned down a lucrative offer to become president of the Rockefeller Foundation in New York. Risk? What risk? Once again, in what would have been a perilous passage for others, the ever-buoyant Mike Pearson was kissed by the winds of fortune.

Of course, there was the little matter of being elected. His biggest opposition here was Maryon, who disliked politics. Another worry was money, should he be defeated one day. But Maryon was persuaded, and the faithful Walter Gordon and other anonymous donors established a "modest" trust fund of $100,000 in Maryon's name to supplement their income. Now all Pearson needed was a riding. No problem there; it would be Algoma East in northwestern Ontario, a party stronghold. The sitting member would be made a senator, a by-election would be called, Pearson would be nominated and elected. And so he was, even if the Liberals had to pull out an electoral map of Ontario to show their cosmopolitan carpetbagger his new constituency.

No one could accuse Pearson of being a natural politician. He never much liked the hustings, then or later. No matter. The retiring MP, the seasoned Tom Farquhar, shepherded Pearson through the churches and social clubs of the sprawling riding, which included Manitoulin Island in Lake Huron and the uranium mines of Elliot Lake. Farquhar taught Pearson the secrets of electioneering, such as waving at anyone he saw from the backseat of the car. Once, when Pearson was waving too vigorously, Farquhar deadpanned: "You can stop waving now; we're out of the constituency." Mike and Maryon campaigned every day for more than a month. On October 25, 1948, he was elected. His margin (1,236) was the thinnest since Farquhar had first won the riding in 1935. But it was the first of eight consecutive victories in Algoma East. Although Pearson would serve the riding as minister, opposition leader, and prime minister, spending more time in New York than in Meldrum Bay (he once went almost a year without visiting the riding), the electors never held it against him.

WHEN PEARSON BECAME secretary of state for external affairs on September 10, 1948, six weeks before his election to Parliament, he inherited a foreign service that was much bigger than the one he had entered twenty years earlier. In 1939, the department had just six legations employing sixteen officers; in 1948, there were forty-four legations (including the United Nations in New York and Geneva) employing some 216 officers, with many more staff at home. The growth of the department reflected a growth of responsibility. This was no longer a diffident diplomacy for a country content to say nothing; it was a diplomatic service for a country that wanted to show up and speak up. At a time the government was cutting back other departments, External Affairs was expanding, a commitment that seems to be forgotten today as the department again absorbs budget cuts in a country throwing off huge annual surpluses. "This country's foreign policy is largely Pearson-inspired," remarked the *Montreal Standard* on November 13, 1948. That was largely true. Now the department would be Pearson-presided. He was choreographer, director, and producer.

For the next nine years, until the Liberals lost power in 1957, this would be Pearson's show. So significant was his contribution in this decade that even had he never become prime minister, his life would still have been considered an unquestionable success. Diplomacy would have been his monument. It was here, in the 1950s, that his star shone brightest. As chair of international bodies, including president of the UN General Assembly in 1952–53, he was swept into the eddies and whirlpools of international crises and asked to find a way out. It was here, in one maelstrom after another, that he developed what became known as Pearsonian Diplomacy.

Distilling events, we see how Pearson used agility, imagination, patience, and empathy—all qualities of the diplomat that he had in great supply—to cool tensions and advance peace. As the world split between East and West, as decolonization dismantled old empires and the United States displaced Great Britain, there was a call for cool heads and experienced hands. Pearson had both. In the establishment of NATO, he ensured that Canada was the first, or among the first, to give voice to a regional pact. When the twelve member states gathered in Washington to sign the North Atlantic Treaty on April 4, 1949, they established an alliance that would help keep the peace in a divided Europe during the Cold War. NATO would be among many roles Canada had in a starring season on the world stage, as the country contributed in big ways and small to the world's new institutional architecture.

The British Commonwealth of Nations, which grew out of the British Empire, twice engaged the attentions of Pearson early in his tenure as minister. The first time was in 1949, when India, having won its independence two years earlier, decided to become a republic. The question was whether, no longer having any link to the monarchy, India could remain in the Commonwealth. Australia and New Zealand balked; Canada sought a compromise. A

Commonwealth heads of government meeting was called for London in April 1949. With an election to be held that June, Louis St. Laurent declined to go and sent Pearson in his place. He was the senior spokesman for Canada, the senior member of the Commonwealth. The meeting lasted six days. Once again, Pearson helped broker a compromise that led to a change he called "one of the most important landmarks in the history of the Commonwealth." India would recognize the role of the monarchy in the Commonwealth, but not in India itself; it would have no king. Because of the change, the Commonwealth reconstituted itself, admitting new members from Africa and Asia and becoming a multilateral, multiracial organization.

Pearson faced a second momentous decision in the Commonwealth the next year. The occasion was a meeting of the foreign ministers in Colombo, the capital of Ceylon (now Sri Lanka), which took place in January 1950. The foreign ministers met for a fortnight and committed their countries to help the peoples of the southern hemisphere lift themselves out of poverty. The Colombo Plan, as it was called, was the world's first aid program for the developing world. Pearson was sympathetic but unenthusiastic, as was St. Laurent. Giving away money was a new concept to a pinched Canada in 1950, poorer, relatively, than it is today.

Pearson also worried about the effectiveness of the plan and whether Canada could afford it, being the only non-sterling nation. But just as NATO was a bulwark against communism in Europe, economic development, in Pearson's view, was a bulwark against communism in Asia. And as the process gained momentum, his enthusiasm grew. Escott Reid, an early supporter, recalls how Pearson struggled, almost single-handedly, to persuade his colleagues, including St. Laurent, that foreign aid was the future. Cabinet met six times to discuss the question. The meetings, recalled Douglas LePan, Pearson's economic adviser, were "difficult and contentious," some of them "stormy in the extreme." On February 15, 1951, Pearson announced that the government had agreed to commit $25 million (U.S.) a year for six years. Reid called it the most revolutionary of changes in Canada's foreign policy, an aid program driven by little more than anti-communism and an idea of a multiracial Commonwealth. Yet Colombo marked the beginning of Canada's program of international assistance, which would, for a period, make it social worker to the world.

SIX MONTHS AFTER PEARSON RETURNED from Colombo, fighting broke out in Korea. The expectation in 1950 was that war would come in Europe, not in Asia, and it underscored the necessity, said Pearson, of assuring the peoples of the East of "our interest, our sympathy and our support." Economic development would take time. Meanwhile, Pearson worried about the escalating tensions on the Korean peninsula—actually the first conflict of the Cold War— which threatened to bring the United States on to the battlefield against China. When the Communists crossed the thirty-eighth parallel and entered South Korea on June 25, Pearson thought it was a civil war. He didn't expect the United States to intervene, and he didn't see Korea as a question of collective security. But when the United States announced on June 27 that it would send forces to Korea, and the Security Council asked the members of the United Nations to help "restore international peace and security to the area," Pearson agreed. When the resolution was passed, the Soviets were out of the room, so there was reason to doubt the spirit of collective security. But once the United Nations was involved, Pearson instinctively thought Canada should be too. For him, it was critical for this to be a collective police action under the authority of the United Nations, which Geoffrey Pearson called "the leitmotif of Canadian policy in the months ahead."

As its contribution to the proposed UN force, Canada offered transport planes and three destroyers. Pearson worried that this would be an American force, and made the first of his entreaties to Washington—which would define his effort here—to accept a "UN commander" and the concept of "UN forces." It refused, and placed the force under the command of General Douglas MacArthur. Because the Canadian Army numbered only about twenty thousand at the time, Canada had limited resources to offer after Britain, Australia, and New Zealand said they would send troops. Pearson suggested establishing a volunteer brigade, inviting member states to earmark a part of their military for the United Nations. Eventually, Canada did this, joined by a few others. Over the next three years, Canada sent 26,791 soldiers to Korea and suffered 516 deaths.

The war was becoming dangerous. Having made a spectacular landing at Inchon in September, MacArthur had pushed the North Koreans over the thirty-eighth parallel and was driving toward the Yalu River, which separated Korea from Manchuria. The South Koreans and Americans crossed in October, the Chinese counterattacked and repulsed them. Pearson feared that if there were a war with the Chinese, the Korea mission would no longer be an exercise in collective security. As Pearson and others saw it, there was a division between the military ends pursued by MacArthur and the political ends espoused by Washington, which was unable or unwilling to control him. In November, MacArthur had launched an assault "to end the war," which brought a Chinese response, ending in a stalemate on the thirty-eighth parallel that lasted until the armistice in July 1953. As Canadian forces were arriving in mid-December, tensions were rising. "Apocalypse was in the air," said Geoffrey Pearson.

The only response, Pearson thought, was to try to bring the war to an end. In December he was asked to serve with representatives of India and Iran on a three-member ceasefire committee established by the General Assembly. They agreed on principles for a ceasefire and hoped to bring along China, but then the Americans introduced a resolution in the General Assembly in early 1951 that called the Chinese the "aggressor." Pearson's response shows his deft diplomacy. He agreed with the sentiments—the *Chinese* were aggressors to him—but worried that the impact of the resolution would be to make the Chinese even more intransigent. As political scientist Denis Stairs reminds us, he also did not believe in empty gestures. Posturing had its uses, but not here. When it came to voting on the resolution, which Pearson called "premature and unwise," he voted in favour. He did so reluctantly but artfully, to preserve his stature with the Americans, whose respect he would need in the future. The war went on for two more years, but the settlement looked much like what the commission had proposed. Along the way, Pearson mediated effectively but delicately between Dean Acheson and Krishna Menon on the repatriation of prisoners.

In 1952, Pearson was elected president of the Seventh Session of the General Assembly, with the support of fifty-one of sixty members. Neither his personal esteem nor the prestige of his office was enough to move the United States or the other side toward a settlement on Korea, but Pearson kept trying. He never broke with the United States, but he privately feared that MacArthur's aggressiveness would trump Truman's authority. His fears crystallized in a highly publicized speech he gave in Toronto on April 10, 1951, in which he warned that the United Nations must not be a servant of the United States and that Washington was not beyond criticism. "It would also help if the United States took more notice of what we do and, indeed, occasionally, of what we say." Then, memorably, he added: "The days of relatively easy and automatic political relations with our neighbour are, I think, over." They were, and Korea was the first rupture.

It is easy to say, as some historians do, that Canada sided too quickly with the United States, did its bidding too often, wasn't independent enough. But Pearson worried greatly about American excesses as the world's lone atomic power and tried to contain them. He was so persistently skeptical of the Americans that his attitude strained his friendship with Acheson, who came to dismiss those "moralizing, interfering Canadians." Acheson never forgave Pearson. Pulling the tail of the eagle was always risky—but Canada was respected and so was Pearson. It is no shame, and some praise, to call his modus operandi "the diplomacy of constraint." In Korea, his foremost impulse was to moderate American power. In doing so—prodding, pushing, petitioning—he became the image of Canada as broker and fixer.

Pearson's stature was rising. *Saturday Night* called him "the most widely known Canadian who has ever existed." In 1954, in Geneva, he worked for peace in Indochina after Canada had joined the International Control Commission organized to supervise the settlement. In 1955, he met the animated Nikita Khrushchev in the Crimea, the first western foreign minister to visit the Soviet Union after Stalin's death. After a night of nineteen toasts of vodka, he gamely said that he had endured "conviviality beyond the line of duty." Later that year, he helped find a compromise admitting sixteen new members to the United Nations. In 1956, he was asked to join a committee of "three wise men" to advise NATO on non-military co-operation and strengthening its unity.

In all things, he saw the big picture. In the spring of 1956, *The New York Times* declared: "Some Britons have accused him of being too pro-United States, and some Americans have said he is too pro-British. The truth is that he is thoroughly pro-Canadian."

CHAPTER SIX

Saving the World

And so we come to Suez, the greatest of the crises—and the greatest of the triumphs—in the statecraft of Lester Pearson. Even with the hindsight of today, this desert imbroglio seems no less dangerous to the peace of the world now than it did then—and Pearson's intervention no less critical to "saving" it, as his admirers would say later. It was an opportunity made for Pearson, drawing on talents forged in a diplomatic career now reaching its zenith. It is as if all his twenty-eight years in diplomacy (including eight as foreign minister) had been but preparation for those tumultuous days in the autumn of 1956. Nothing before or after was as momentous for him. In his long, eventful public life, Suez was his signature.

Always conscious of the credibility of a young United Nations, Pearson had been watching things worsen in the Middle East in the mid-1950s. When Gamal Abdel Nasser, the president of Egypt, nationalized the Suez Canal Company on July 26, 1956, he lit a fuse. On October 29, the Israelis, with British and French support, reacted by attacking Egypt. Pearson was caught entirely by surprise. He was angry and incredulous when Anthony Eden, the British prime minister, had the audacity to ask for Canada's "understanding" and "support" for the Anglo-French effort "to ensure the safety of the Suez Canal." Pearson was staggered that Eden, with whom he had played tennis in their days at the League of Nations in the 1930s, could be so reckless. There would be no support or understanding from Canada. To Pearson, the action was immoral (against international law), impractical (the British and French could not hold the canal long against insurgents), and incendiary (splitting the Anglo-American alliance and dividing the Commonwealth along racial lines). Eden had ignored the United Nations and antagonized his allies. Had he gone mad?

The United States introduced a motion in the Security Council calling for a ceasefire and withdrawal of all troops. Britain and France vetoed it. The issue then went to an emergency session of the General Assembly, where no nation had a veto. That was called for Thursday, November 1. In Ottawa, St. Laurent formally replied to Eden in "regret more than anger," as Geoffrey Pearson recalls, though Uncle Louis was less than avuncular. Then Pearson flew to New York on a government airplane, where he sat alone in silence. Bruce

Hutchison, who accompanied him as a journalist, wrote: "He knew that for the first time a Canadian might hold in his hand the peace of the world and, with a little luck, might save it."

Five days before, the Soviets had sent their tanks into Hungary to put down a rebellion, an act that had stunned the West. Now, while Israeli bombs were falling on Port Said, the Soviets warned darkly of sending help to the Egyptians. The Americans were angry. The Commonwealth was divided, with India threatening to leave. The French franc and British pound were trembling. And the world was watching. "On television, that Suez spectacle was the Watergate hearing of its day," recalled Geoffrey Murray, then the senior counsellor in Canada's UN mission, in 1973. "New Yorkers even forgot for a while to push and yell and claw at each other, so intently were they watching the tube flicker and flash the faces of speakers on the podium, the huddles around national desks, the scampering to and fro of bagmen and arm-twisters." At the United Nations, the galleries were full, the lights ablaze, the bar in the North Lounge (where Walter, the bartender, mixed excellent whisky sours) running full tilt. It was the worst crisis since the Korean War, and again, the United Nations was its epicentre. Suez was playing on the main stage, Hungary in the theatre next door.

Consider the scene when Pearson entered the General Assembly on the afternoon of November 1. France and Britain, Canada's mother countries, were in a shooting war that Canada condemned. The United States, Canada's neighbour and ally, was trying to restrain them. Everyone wanted a way out. Pearson, who had kept Canada uncommitted and an ally to all three, was uniquely positioned to find it. John Holmes, a junior diplomat at the mission who was with Pearson in the great hall that day, recalled, "People kept rushing up to me ... and they would say, 'What's he got? We hear Mike's got a proposal? It's high time. Can he do it?'" It was as if Pearson was Moses with his people before the Red Sea, or, in this case, the Suez Canal, contemplating a way across. However he went, he knew that Canada was caught in the cross-currents of its three closest friends.

How to part the waters and save the day? First, abstain on the American resolution of that evening calling for a cease-fire (unlike Australia and New Zealand, which voted against). Offend no one. Then, having remained silent during the debate, explain why. Say nice things about your ancestors ("two countries which have contributed so much to man's progress and freedom under the law"). Sound reasonable. Hopeful. Sympathetic. Pearson's main worry was that the U.S. resolution was incomplete, making no mention of a peace conference and a settlement, which he thought necessary to allow the British and the French to save face. He knew there was no time to amend it that evening. So, after the resolution passed overwhelmingly, Pearson went straight to the podium to urge the Assembly to authorize "a United Nations police force large enough to keep these borders at peace while a political settlement is being worked out." To this contingent, Canada offered its own troops.

There it was then. Canada had not only made the proposal, it had offered boots on the ground. John Foster Dulles, the U.S. secretary of state, followed Pearson to the podium and applauded his initiative. So did Britain and France, which badly wanted a solution, looking longingly to Pearson to get them "off the hook." Pearson returned to Ottawa, asked cabinet to approve the idea, and returned to New York for a second session on Saturday, November 3. At midnight, he introduced a motion authorizing the Secretary-General to create an emergency international force to supervise a cease-fire. Strictly speaking, that motion was not his. It was written in Washington and handed to Pearson by the American ambassador, Henry Cabot Lodge, who stepped out of his small office and saw Pearson in the corridor. Lodge could not introduce the motion himself (it would be seen as imperialist) and was looking for another country to act as a sponsor.

"There was Mike Pearson coming through the door toward me and I decided then and there that he was the one; he was going to get it if he wanted it." Had it not been Pearson, Lodge added later, he was going to approach Ambassador João Carlos Muniz of Brazil, though surely Lodge felt that it had to be Pearson, the most seasoned professional in the place. Lodge knew there was no one at the United Nations who could have made up his mind faster and understood the problem better. "It was the quickest thing I have ever seen in my life," he recalled of how Pearson took the motion, read it, and introduced it—all in a matter of minutes. "It was remarkable—one of the high points of my political life." The debate over the resolution went into Sunday. More consulting, conferring, cajoling. At 2:00 a.m., the resolution passed 57–0, with 19 abstentions, including the Soviets. Delegates rushed to the podium to congratulate Pearson. Not even Britain had opposed the resolution, although it would allow Nasser, whom Eden compared to Hitler, to remain in place.

But the peacekeeping force had to be assembled quickly. Time was short; to maintain the pressure, the British armada was sailing to Egypt. Pearson met with Secretary-General Dag Hammarskjöld and delegates from India, Colombia, and Norway. By November 5, a force had been devised, to be led by General E.L.M. Burns, a Canadian. On the same day, British and French paratroopers landed in Port Said. On November 7, a ceasefire was declared. On November 15, UN soldiers arrived. The Israelis withdrew, the canal reopened, the crisis passed. Establishing a peace in the coming months would proceed by fits and starts, but there was no shooting. Canada would contribute a thousand soldiers to the force standing between Arabs and Israelis, though not drawn from the Queen's Own (who fly the Red Ensign), whom the Egyptians rejected as British proxies.

At the centre of the whirlwind was the master of events, the imperturbable Lester Pearson. It was he who made or modified the proposals, presented the critical resolutions, enlisted support, persuaded skeptics. How did he carry it off? After years at the United Nations, he knew the General Assembly, its rules, rhythms, and personalities (most by first name) and they knew him. In June 1956, *The New York Times* had called Pearson "sui generis ... one of the few Canadians whose name, and lectures, are known around the world." He knew that both sides had to find victory in a resolution and that flexibility was key. But what is also important, when we revisit this drama a half-century later, is to appreciate what he did not do. For Pearson, we should remember, success at Suez was less the idea than the *instinct*. The peacekeeping force had many mothers—it had been proposed or raised as a concept by others, including Lodge and even Anthony Eden in London on the same day Pearson introduced it—but it needed a midwife. This was more about tactics than strategy. Process mattered. So did patience, forbearance, stamina. Geoffrey Murray watched Pearson that first night in the General Assembly writing his statement near the floodlit podium, amazed as he "scribbled notes ... frequently interrupted by urgent consultations and messages, always in the din of debate." Fortunately, Pearson did not have to reconcile intransigent parties. The British and French wanted a graceful exit, and no more so than when their currencies began to fall and the Americans threatened economic retaliation. With countries that wanted to be saved from themselves, Pearson did not have to do much arm-twisting. His persistence and perception carried the day and produced the resolution. In the eyes of the antagonists, a misstep or misstatement could have turned our floor manager into a four-flusher. It all could have gone terribly wrong, but it didn't. No single event before or since in his public service would surpass Suez. It was Lester Pearson's finest hour.

At home, though, public opinion was so divided that some argue (not always persuasively) that it cost the Liberals the election the following June. As foreign minister, Pearson had always managed to avoid being the subject of partisan attacks. Now the Conservatives thought Pearson disloyal; indeed, it was the first time in its history that Canada had not supported the British at war. Howard Green, a future foreign minister, called Pearson "a chore boy for the United States" and growled that Suez was "the most disgraceful period in the country's history." His intervention represented the Americanization of Canada, the abandonment of the Mother Country. "It is high time that Canada had a government which will not knife Canada's best friends in the back," he said. W. Earl Rowe, the acting opposition leader, declared: "Let not the government believe it can deceive the Canadian people by creating a fancy halo around the Secretary of State for External Affairs, as if he already saved the world's peace and solved the Suez Canal crisis."

Little did Rowe know that he was writing the citation of the Nobel Peace Prize that Pearson would win the next year. When a reporter called Pearson with news of the prize on October 14, 1957, he was told he must be mistaken. When the reporter confirmed and called back, Pearson said, "Gosh!" The Nobel Committee called Suez "a victory for the UN and for the man who contributed more than anyone else to save the world at that time." At home, not everyone cheered. A woman at a cocktail party in Vancouver is said to have announced, perhaps apocryphally: "Mike Pearson has won the Nobel Prize! Well, who does he think *he* is?" John Diefenbaker seethed that Pearson had stolen his thunder on the day the Queen was opening Parliament. For years, he muttered that Pearson should never have won the prize.

More than any other honour—and there were many in his career—the Nobel Prize gave Pearson that enduring halo. It made him something else, something beyond himself. Canadians respect foreign honours more than their own—and none more than this one. Its lustre grew slowly though. While it helped him become leader of the Liberal Party in 1958, it wasn't enough to make him prime minister later that year. Eventually, though, the Nobel Prize conferred a kind of holy legitimacy on the man. In the last quarter-century, in particular, peacekeeping has become a part of our iconography, celebrated on a postage stamp, the ten-dollar bill, and in an imposing stone monument on Sussex Drive in Ottawa. Many Canadians have come to see Canada exclusively as a peacekeeper, as if there is a rare property in our national psyche—perhaps an instinct for accommodation, a unique gene of tolerance or compromise—that makes us a natural at this task. It has become a touchstone of our identity.

From Suez came a mythology that Pearson believed peacekeeping was Canada's international vocation. It wasn't so. Yes, Canada did become the world's leading peacekeeper, for years contributing as much as 10 percent of the UN forces. It served for a decade in the Sinai and almost three decades in Cyprus and a host of other places, where, together with other countries, it stood on a border between combatants. Until 1989, Canada never refused a request from the United Nations to take on a mission. Important as it was, though, peacekeeping was always a relatively small part of Canada's international military obligations, far outweighed by our commitment to NATO. Today, Canada has largely withdrawn from peacekeeping (which, it should be said, is no longer what it was). Once the world's leading contributor, we are now fifty-third among nations.

But if we have withdrawn from peacekeeping, or our idea of peacekeeping, it has not withdrawn from us. When Canadians are asked about Afghanistan, where scores of Canadian soldiers have died in combat, they think that Canada is there because this is a peacekeeping mission—or that Canada should not be there because it isn't. In a way, Pearson's finding a solution to Suez was the worst thing that could have happened to Canada and to its most famous diplomat. Pearson became synonymous with peace. It turned him into a do-gooder, a pacifist on the mountaintop, a saffron-robed priest. His granddaughter Anne Pearson says this is the reason that she is "a Baha'i, whose teachings are similar to what Lester Pearson espoused." She also thinks that it is "paradoxical" that Pearson could have helped establish NATO. Today, were he here, he would explain that the purpose of NATO was to keep the peace and protect western democracy. Suez coloured that commitment. In a sense it denied the history of Canada, which keeps peace when it can but fights when it must, as it did in three big wars in the twentieth century, at a cost of some one hundred thousand Canadians who fell in foreign fields.

Saving the world? I was just doing my job, said Mike.

SUEZ WAS A HIGH-WATER MARK for Lester Pearson, as politician or public servant. Nothing he did as foreign minister surpassed it; indeed, some suggest that nothing he did as prime minister surpassed it. Well, perhaps. If Suez marked the acme of his diplomacy, though, it also marked its end. Seven months later, he was out of power.

How did he do it? Pearsonian Diplomacy has come to mean a modus operandi. Pearson had a capacity for cooling off a situation, as he tried to do in Korea. He also had an instinct for creating a middle way, as he did with India and the Commonwealth in 1949, another one of those intractable conflicts. "I was in a rather easy position as this was a battle that could be left to other delegations who took extreme views on one side or the other and my efforts could be devoted to finding a compromise between the extremes," he said of that impasse. In Kashmir in 1950, though, he knew to stay away; the issue was insoluble, and he had no appetite for lost causes. In Hungary, in 1956, he knew not to try to replicate his success at Suez, because that would be considered overreaching for a country of Canada's size. As Denis Stairs points out, Pearson knew the limits. You could have influence, on a good day, but you shouldn't expect it every day.

What were the human elements of Pearson's diplomacy? Patience, empathy, and the ability to understand another's reality. All would serve him well. Endurance for those nocturnal sessions. Vision. Patience. Strategic silence. An ability to evade, equivocate, obfuscate. A sense of humour. Always.

The statecraft of the 1940s and 1950s would become known as "the golden age of Canadian diplomacy." This term was popularized by Pearson's colleagues and contemporaries, those generalist-gentlemen of the department. Having made history, they then wrote it—in the memoirs, chronicles, and diaries of Escott Reid, George Ignatieff, Douglas LePan, Hugh Keenleyside, Charles Ritchie, John Holmes, and Pearson himself. All celebrate Canada's contribution. While none of the writers take personal cred-it—self-advertisement was not their way—they take pride in what Canada did in the world. While some say this era start-ed in the early 1940s, before Pearson became minister, it is so closely identified with him that it came to be named for him.

The revisionists say that it was never thus. They deny that Canada has declined in the world, an argument made in the lean years before and after the start of the new millennium. "Decline?" they ask. "Decline from what?" They do not think that Canada has stepped away from its spirited inter-nationalism—a quantitative as much as a qualitative differ-ence—because they deny that it was as glorious as the golden-agers described it. Historian Greg Donaghy argues that the records of the 1940s and 1950s show that Canada's diplomats were little different than Mackenzie King in their appreciation of *realpolitik* and the necessity of Canada's "modest" role. "Conscious of limited means, they were inclined to shun burdensome international responsibilities, followers not leaders," he wrote in an essay called "Coming off the Gold Standard." Their diplomacy was cautious and pragmatic.

Donaghy's argument is that we weren't what we think we were. We didn't do that much in the creation of the United

Nations, where Australia was more articulate; we were slow to come to the aid of South Korea and practised an uncreative diplomacy there; we exaggerated our role at Suez; we made too much of Article 2 and the Atlantic Community and didn't exercise much influence at NATO; we waffled on the Colombo Plan and were slow to ante up for aid. It is a sorry tale of how we spoke in the poetry of idealism but acted in the prose of realism. It fooled a whole generation. Worse than disappointing, it is dangerous today, you see, because it raises expectations that governments cannot meet. Alas, friends, it was really the Age of Bronze. Time to abandon that gold standard.

There is some truth to this line of argument. There were real disappointments in the postwar era, in the Commonwealth, NATO, and foreign aid. There was timidity. But the argument is so deliciously Canadian, consistent with the narrowing horizons of a country that has allowed the arms of its internationalism—diplomacy, development, and defence—to erode calamitously in the last generation. The argument is that we really didn't do great things in the past—at least not as much as we said—and therefore we need not hold ourselves to a higher standard today. It is neo-colonial: think small.

Pearson never thought small. He ridiculed King's timidity and refused to serve in his cabinet. He was never one of his disciples, which is why King had gnawing reservations about his activist deputy. Pearson was always pushing, thinking, imagining. The diplomacy of constraint in Korea was not a reflection of paralysis but of agility. The diplomacy of accommodation saved the day at Suez. In both crises, Canada played roles that would have been unimaginable in the 1930s. Pearson was slow on aid but embraced it, and Canada's early annual commitment—$25 million—was respectable. If Canada was so ineffective in these years, why did the world look to Canada at Suez? Why did Canada become the world's leading peacekeeper? Why did it become one of the world's leading donors? And why was it voted on to the Security Council every decade? So diminished is our stature today that Canada may not take its traditional two-year turn on the Security Council in the first decade of the new century.

If the golden age was dross, though, the statesmanship of Lester Pearson was luminous. It was no accident that he was elected president of the General Assembly and twice came within a veto of becoming Secretary-General. He was offered the directorship of the FAO and the Secretary-Generalship of NATO. He was a member of the Korean ceasefire committee in 1950 and one of the "three wise men" in 1956. Suez was his greatest moment, but it was one of many. Once he left diplomacy for politics, the applause from afar would never again be as long and as loud, for him and for Canada.

CHAPTER SEVEN

The Wilderness Campaign

It is unclear when Lester Pearson decided that he wanted to become leader of the Liberal Party. Some of his associates maintained that he expressed an interest as early as the late 1940s, but kept quiet because it was unsporting to show too much ambition in Canada. Certainly others were speculating about his plans. In 1948, only two months after he became foreign minister, the *Montreal Standard* mused that "the prime ministership may well be what Pearson wants." In 1950, two newspaper polls named him Man of the Year. The next year, *New Liberty* suggested that he might run for the leadership and predicted: "If he does, he will be hard to beat." And *Maclean's* reported that "he's now rated the likeliest Liberal to succeed Prime Minister St. Laurent." Pearson insisted that he had no desire for the job—as he said of almost all the jobs in his career. In 1970, he called the decision to run for the leadership "the most difficult one I had ever to make." If so, it appears that he wasn't brooding on a mountaintop to the swells of Beethoven's *Seventh Symphony*. In fact, he didn't seem to have taken it seriously until the leadership became vacant in September 1957, three months after the Conservatives had defeated the Liberals, ending their twenty-two years in power. If Pearson did want the job, those disavowals notwithstanding, he showed no enthusiasm. When he was asked to visit the ailing St. Laurent at his summer home in Quebec to solicit the leader's intentions, Pearson invited Lionel Chevrier, his former cabinet colleague, to come along so that no one could say that Pearson was trying to push out St. Laurent, as Anthony Eden had Churchill in 1955. Implausibly, Pearson hoped that the seventy-five-year-old St. Laurent would stay on. Even when the party set its leadership convention for mid-January, it wasn't clear that Pearson would run. "He wasn't terribly keen about it," recalled Robert Fowler, a friend and prominent Liberal. "He, however, more or less accepted the inevitable." Pearson told Fowler and Walter Gordon: "Well, I will accept this if it comes along. I'm not going to scratch for it."

Scratch for it. Ultimately, he didn't have to scratch for it; he didn't have to do much at all. He became leader of the party with the same kind of shrug with which he'd become foreign minister. Again, the office sought him more than he sought the office. His effortless ascent continued. As the party had wooed him in 1948—offering a senior portfolio, arranging financial security, fixing up a safe seat—so it wooed him for the leadership. Again, Pearson's timing was perfect. The Liberals had alternated between French and English leaders since Edward Blake (Laurier, King, St. Laurent) and now it was an anglophone's turn. By then, though, the giants of the day—Douglas Abbott, Brooke Claxton, C.D. Howe, Walter Harris—were gone. Paul Martin Sr., who coveted the job even more than he had in 1948, was seen as a French Catholic. It was another reason that Pearson, the English Protestant, was heir apparent. Any doubt dissolved in October when he won the Nobel Prize. Still, Walter Gordon had to persuade Pearson to mount a campaign and put together an organization. They spent only $3,000, and Gordon covered it personally. Pearson declared his candidacy to a reporter on December 4, almost by accident. "I didn't do anything," he said later of his campaign. No matter. When delegates voted on January 16, 1958, he had 1,074 votes and Martin had 305 votes. Once again, the party had taken care of things.

The out-of-power Liberals could not make Pearson prime minister immediately—not that they weren't working on it. Such was their presumption that Jack Pickersgill, the veteran minister and party strategist, could advise Pearson to move a motion of non-confidence in the government four days after he became leader. It would accuse the Conservatives, who had been elected with seven more seats, of being unfit to govern. The ploy was to force the Conservatives from power without forcing an election. Surely John Diefenbaker, who had run for public office five times unsuccessfully before entering Parliament, would graciously yield to the Leader of the Opposition, Nobel Laureate, and saviour of the world? Surely he would agree that the Liberals, having emerged from six agonizing months in purgatory, should reclaim what was rightfully theirs under St. Mike of Suez? Surely the country would recognize its mistake and return to its senses?

Diefenbaker, the fiercest of partisans, was gleeful. For two hours he eviscerated Pearson in the House of Commons. He wouldn't go to the Governor General to ask the Liberals to form a government, as his opponents had hoped. Instead, Diefenbaker called an election for March 31. Pearson wasn't ready. Neither was his party. St. Laurent went to Florida and seemed to take all the professionals with him. The campaign was "the most exhausting, frustrating eight weeks of my life," Pearson said. When it began—and even as it ended— the fledgling leader had no appreciation of the looming disaster. Sure, he might lose, but how bad could it be? Bad. Very bad. The Conservatives won 208 seats in the House of Commons, the largest number in parliamentary history. The Liberals won 49 seats, the smallest number in their history. Worse, they had been reduced to a rump in central Canada and had no seats in the West. As Maryon surveyed the wreckage that evening, horrified by the prospect of her husband leading a ragtag opposition, she delivered her memorable blow upon a bruise: *You've lost everything, Mike. You've even won your seat.*

The party had been devastated. Surely it would take two or three elections to dislodge the Conservative government. In the spring of 1958, Pearson was sixty-one. An optimist might have seen his fate as exile to Elba, promising early escape; a realist would have seen it as exile to St. Helena, denying any escape. Pearson had reasons for self-doubt. First, he was essentially new to politics; although he had been in Parliament for almost ten years, as foreign minister, he had been insulated. His first taste of partisanship was the Suez Crisis, and it had wounded him. Second, he thought himself temperamentally unsuited to politics. His world was diplomacy, where the instinct is to accommodate rather than destroy an opponent. "Maryon thinks I am too disgustingly sporting to be any good at politics," he wrote Margaret

Ryan, a friend, in 1958. In diplomacy, flexibility is an asset. Victory is compromise. In politics, flexibility is weakness. Victory is total. Besides, Pearson wasn't a populist. Charming and funny as he was in small groups, he was no glad-hander, backslapper, or baby-kisser. He was too shy. Asked once to shake the hands of a group of homeless people, he refused; he couldn't "exploit their suffering." Nor was he a stump speaker. They could get him out of his polka-dot bow ties, soften the subtle lisp, change the words, but he was still more Elmer Fudd than Cicero. And he certainly wasn't Diefenbaker, who despite his bombast (or perhaps because of it) was an electrifying orator and formidable campaigner. The contrast would become sharper when John F. Kennedy became president in 1961. Pearson was twenty years older than the vigorous Kennedy, the first president born in the twentieth century. Pearson was born in the nineteenth century and looked and sounded like it.

Yes, it would have been tempting to walk away after the calamity in 1958. Some thought he would and should. By the next election, Pearson would be the age of retirement. Maryon wanted him home. He had options. For all that, though, he decided to stay. Today the decision wouldn't be his alone; Tories and Grits give leaders only one chance to win. But in the 1950s, when the system was less presidential and politics more loyal, leaders ran and ran and ran. Pearson was elected in 1963 on his third attempt (after losing elections in 1958 and 1962). Diefenbaker lost twice (1963, 1965) after winning three times (1957, 1958, 1962).

That Pearson stayed showed his tenacity and sense of duty. He could not know that the Conservatives would self-destruct, squandering their majority in four years. By the summer of 1958, without any such hope to sustain him, the leader of Her Majesty's Loyal Opposition was oddly content. "Since the debacle of March 31, I have really worked very hard—as hard as I have ever worked—and believe it or not I'm rather enjoying my new role as irresponsible critic and general opposer," he wrote Margaret Ryan in July. "It's like going back to school again...."

In a sense it was. After nearly destroying the party, he set about remaking it. He not only had to go back to school, he had to build a new one, hire teachers, design courses, attract students. As a bureaucrat, Pearson was an indifferent administrator. Yet here, in an entirely new enterprise, he was startlingly effective. The resurrection of the Liberal Party between 1958 and 1963 is the least recognized achievement of his life. The party could have wandered in the wilderness for a decade. Its exile was shorter because Pearson recruited smart people, produced good policy, and showed sound instincts. It was all that, of course—and the good fortune of facing a blundering government apparently determined to lose the confidence of Canadians.

The Conservatives did not fall apart right away. That took time. Diefenbaker, a superior and nastier parliamentarian, vilified Pearson daily, and it shook him. One day Pearson returned from a long weekend of reflection and told Lionel Chevrier: "I have decided to stick to the job. I do not care what Diefenbaker says about me. I intend to ignore him completely and go about my duties as efficiently as I can." He did. He had promised a program of "a free and independent Canadianism, not narrow nationalism," and he would deliver one. The fact that he attracted the right people wasn't an accident; they were drawn to Pearson. "I don't think I have ever met a man with greater courage, moral strength or capacity to secure loyalty from his followers than Mike Pearson," gushed Chevrier. In these years, Pearson recruited Tom Kent, a former English newspaperman; Mitchell Sharp, a former public servant; and Keith Davey, a spirited advertising executive. There was also Maurice Lamontagne and Allan MacEachen, economists both, and later Richard O'Hagan, a former journalist. The point man was Walter Gordon, Pearson's old friend and consigliere, who was assiduously modernizing the party organization.

These were thinkers, strategists, publicists, mechanics. At the same time, Pearson was attracting a constellation of candidates who would dominate national politics for years to come—Bud Drury, Jean Chrétien, Lucien Lamoureux, Maurice Sauvé, John Turner, Herb Gray, Eugene Whelan, Donald Macdonald, Pauline Jewett.

Two events were critical to reviving the Liberals. At the Kingston Conference in September 1960, the party invited innovative proposals for economic and social reform from two hundred leading thinkers, who weren't necessarily Liberals. It became a seedbed of ideas. At the National Rally, a policy convention in Ottawa in January 1961, many of these were adopted. Some eighteen hundred partisans assembled for three days to decide what the new government would do in power. "Never before or since has there been such an effective participatory process in a federal political party," recalled Tom Kent in 2006. Critics scoffed that these were empty seminars for a party out of power. Actually, they were the pith and substance of its intellectual renewal. The party platforms of 1962 and 1963 were progressive blue-prints for economic and social reform that would produce the Canada Pension Plan, the Canada Assistance Plan, the Guaranteed Income Supplement, and the Medicare Act. They assumed state intervention and public investment.

Slowly, deliberatively, Pearson was recasting an old, venerable institution that had atrophied under St. Laurent in the 1950s. He was also quietly moving the party to the left, where he'd become comfortable. While he had been seen in his years in cabinet as a man of no fixed ideas as much as a man of no fixed address, his instinct was now liberal. As Bruce Hutchison, his confidant, put it: "He stood for the defenceless little man against the great organized power blocs in this age of giantism."

The Liberals were closely watching JFK, who was promising new frontiers in the United States. *The Making of the President*, Theodore White's groundbreaking account of the 1960 presidential campaign, became their manual. They adopted American techniques and hired American pollsters. At home, the Liberals under Jean Lesage had been elected in Quebec in 1960, launching "the Quiet Revolution" of reform and innovation. Pearson saw the appetite for change. He understood the *zeitgeist*.

By 1962, the Conservatives were self-destructing. They had been trailing the Liberals in the polls for two years and the Liberals smelled victory. Once again the Liberals ran a poor campaign—which they did masterfully in each of the four campaigns Pearson waged as leader—and they lost. In a sense, though, they won. In the election of June 18, the

Conservatives fell to 116 seats and the Liberals rose to 99 seats. It was the anniversary of the Battle of Waterloo, and while Diefenbaker wasn't quite the vanquished Napoleon, he was in full retreat. It had taken the Liberals only one election to reduce this unprecedented majority to a minority. As Wellington had said in victory, it was a close-run thing. For the Liberals, it was only a matter of time.

In the interlude between elections, as the government's death rattle grew louder, Pearson contemplated a pair of seminal issues that marked his development as a politician. The first was national unity, which he addressed in the House of Commons on December 17, 1962, in a speech drafted by Maurice Lamontagne. While he brought no original insight to French Canada—he read but did not speak French, he had no close French-Canadian friends, he had lived only in the Anglo-American world—he was struck by the sea change in Quebec. In the two years since he had defeated the Union Nationale, Jean Lesage was setting in train forces that would transform the province from an agrarian, clerical, conservative society to an industrial, secular, and progressive one. To protect and assert the French fact in Quebec through new laws and programs, he was demanding from Ottawa a share of fiscal power and constitutional authority. Pearson, a student of history, sensed that these forces would remake Canada—that is, if they did not destroy it first. Meanwhile, separatism was taking root in the province, and tin-ear English Canadians such as Donald Gordon, the president of Canadian National, could still say there were no qualified French-speaking Canadians to serve on his board of directors. Pearson was deeply worried about these centrifugal forces in Confederation and wanted to find ways to accommodate them. "We are going through another crisis of national unity," he warned. A somnolent country had needed "shock treatment" to understand what was happening in Quebec, he said. "It is now clear to all, I think, that French-speaking Canadians are determined to become directors of their economic and cultural destiny in their own changed and changing society ... they also ask for equal and full opportunity to participate in all federal government services, in which their own language will be fully recognized. This right flows from the equal partnership of confederation." The prevailing view in English-speaking Canada was that the country was English, he explained, except in Quebec, which was French-speaking. In Quebec, there was a broader view, of a bilingual, bicultural country. Pearson said it was no longer acceptable for the two solitudes to live in isolation. Quebecers were determined to be "masters in our own house" and no longer content to be second class.

His solution? Introduce bilingualism in the public service and in education. He proposed a royal commission to examine these questions. This was the first time that Pearson raised the subject, which was his response to the Quiet Revolution. He was the first English-speaking leader to see the mood in Quebec—sensing that the country was changing irrevocably—and the last English-speaking leader to speak only English. It was an astute observation, particularly for someone of his background. Historian Blair Neatby attributes Pearson's awakening to his exposure to Louis St. Laurent, Maurice Lamontagne, and Jean Lesage, with whom he'd served in the 1950s.

Pearson said later that he never made a more important speech in Parliament. Both Tom Kent and Walter Gordon doubted its value but came to embrace its wisdom. "He did it because this was vital to the country," said Gordon; Lamontagne called it "the beginning of a new era in Canada." Pearson's diagnosis and his prescription were applauded in Quebec. It enhanced Pearson's stature there and attracted a new cadre of loyalists. In parts of English Canada, though, he was accused of appeasing the French. Pearson could not know then how his appreciation of the duality of Canada would change the country, where, decades later, parents in Toronto and Calgary would wait hours to register their children in French immersion classes. In 1978, Peter Stursberg called the speech a "Declaration of French Canadian Rights." In 2006, author Graham Fraser would call it "as close as one can find to an 'I have a dream speech' on official bilingualism." It was also an expression of Pearson's foresight.

Three weeks later, Pearson addressed a more topical question: "the tragic confusion" over the government's policy on nuclear weapons in Canada. During the Cuban Missile Crisis in October 1962, Pearson was distressed by the reluctance of the Conservatives to support the United States when it confronted the Soviet Union over its nuclear missiles in Cuba. As Robert Kennedy sniffed, "Canada offers all aid short of help." Pearson now worried about the government's refusal to accept nuclear weapons for Canada's defensive weapons, including the BOMARC missiles, which left them essentially unarmed. "Canada's position was intolerable," he wrote in his memoirs, "or rather the fact that we had no position was intolerable." As a member of NORAD, the continental defence alliance the Conservatives had joined in 1957, Canada agreed to collaborate on continental defence. To that end, it had invested $600 million in equipment. But despite having agreed to accept nuclear weapons from the United States years earlier, the government was now balking. Pearson was aghast. He abhorred nuclear weapons and their deployment in Canada, which had refused to become a nuclear power after the Second World War. But Pearson felt that an agreement is an agreement and vowed to honour it. In doing that, though, he had a problem with the Liberal Party, which was opposed to the acquisition of nuclear weapons in Canada. His only choice was to reverse its position.

Which is what he did. On January 12, 1963, Pearson addressed a party meeting in Scarborough, outside Toronto. He had consulted Paul Hellyer, his defence critic, and some others. But the decision was largely his: if his party formed the government, it would accept nuclear weapons. Walter Gordon was outraged. So was Pierre Trudeau, who famously called Pearson "the defrocked priest of peace" and dismissed thoughts of running as a Liberal that year. Pearson was unfazed. He saw this less as a moral question than a practical one. Canada was a founding member of NATO, which had adopted this strategy. Its arsenal included nuclear weapons. Canada had supplied uranium for them, including some from mines in his riding. If this was the reality, how could Canada refuse nuclear weapons? Better to take them now, he thought, fulfill our treaty obligations, preserve our relations with Washington, and then, quietly, get rid of them.

As much as the decision was practical, it was political. Although Pearson insisted that he was not trying to capitalize on the ideological divisions within the government or pander to public opinion, which seemed to be on his side, his protest was disingenuous. His nephew, the journalist Chris Young, said that Pearson admitted privately to him that the polls *did* matter to him in deciding to reverse party policy. In any case, tactically, his reversal on nuclear weapons was a master stroke. It accentuated the rift within Diefenbaker's minority government, which pitted the minister of external affairs against the minister of national defence, and precipitated its imminent collapse. It also solidified public support behind the surging Liberals. True, the defection of Trudeau (and Jean Marchand) was a loss to his government between 1963 and 1965. But whatever Pearson lost among the intelligentsia in his *virage*, he gained in other quarters. His decision was politically shrewd, and it showed that this Nobel Laureate was no pacifist. He believed in collective security. If that meant nuclear weapons, so be it. But that didn't make him Dr. Strangelove either. He never learned to love the bomb. In fact, he feared it greatly. As so often, he was a realist more than idealist. In the winter of 1963, his stand on nuclear weapons was decisive and sure-footed. Years later, he said that was the moment when he became a politician.

The government fell on February 5 and an election was called for April 8. Once again, the Liberals ran a poor campaign, full of dubious gimmicks, such as creating "a truth squad" to shadow John Diefenbaker and releasing flocks of homing pigeons at rallies. Pearson, though, was developing not just the sensibilities of a politician but the backbone too. When he faced down a hostile audience in Vancouver on April 1, enduring forty-five minutes of hissing and heckling, peas bouncing off the side of his head, he had become someone different. Bruce Hutchison mused that Canadians now saw "a Pearson unknown to them … no sleek diplomat of the drawing-room, a professor of history or a dilettante of economics … a fighting man, and a tough guy.…" Perhaps so, but for him this wasn't the politics of joy. Pearson called the campaign "the most degrading experience of my life."

Still, he had arrived. After five years in opposition, absorbing the blows of a relentless adversary, reorganizing a moribund party, drafting policy, and recruiting candidates, he had turned a Conservative majority into a Liberal minority. His political apprenticeship was over; he had become a seasoned warrior. He had redeemed his honour. He had kept his promise. He had scratched for it.

CHAPTER EIGHT

Pearson's Canada

Lester Pearson did not start out life promising to be prime minister, unlike his perfervid antagonist, John Diefenbaker, who announced his candidacy in the womb and entered the world campaigning. Pearson was always the reluctant partisan, and he could be as long as he was foreign minister. His leisurely promenade in politics ended rudely in 1958 when he inherited, with little mirth, the leadership of the Liberal Party and promptly marched it into the Anteroom of Death. For five years, he toiled in the marches of the big, sparse country. Little by little, he revived the party and imagined a Liberal Restoration.

He became the fourteenth prime minister of Canada on April 22, 1963. He turned sixty-six the next day. In a time men retired at sixty-five and reliably died within three years, Pearson might have been collecting his pension. Politically, age was an advantage then. Today a party apparatchik in his forties can become prime minister with no ministerial or managerial experience and a summer in politics. In the

1960s, that was unlikely. Leaders were more grey. In April 1963, John Diefenbaker was sixty-seven. Nikita Khrushchev and Harold Macmillan were sixty-nine. Charles de Gaulle was seventy-two. Konrad Adenauer was eighty-seven.

What had sustained Pearson in the wilderness? Surely he had nothing to prove; he had already written the first line of his obituary as foreign minister. He didn't have a cause; he wasn't a creature of causes, lost or otherwise. If Pierre Trudeau entered politics to keep Quebec in Canada, Pearson had no such *idée fixe*. Power wasn't his spur either, as it was for Brian Mulroney or Jean Chrétien. Put it down to a Methodist's sense of duty. Staying on in 1958 was also a matter of pride, even atonement, for his hubris in January. He hadn't become the leader of the Liberal Party of Canada to preside over its demise.

And yet for a man who wasn't by instinct an innovator, he would lead an innovative government. There would be scandal and malfeasance aplenty. To journalists gorging on leaks and missteps, his ministry would be an open bar and bottomless buffet. "The Pearson period ... was more like the voyage of some peeling, once-proud, now leaky excursion steamer, lurching from port to port, with the captain making up his schedule as he went along, too busy keeping afloat to spend much time on the bridge," Peter C. Newman wrote in *The Distemper of Our Times* in 1968, the definitive contemporary account of Pearson's government, reprised in his memoir, *Here Be Dragons*, in 2004.

Forty years later, though, we see the captain and the vessel in a different light. The destination was more important than the voyage. True, the skies darkened, the seas raged, the engines seized. The captain left the bridge, but he never ran aground, never faced mutiny, never lost his way. He steered the ship of state through uncharted waters and found safe harbour. Today the government of the Right Honourable Lester B. Pearson looks surprisingly experimental and singularly transformative. It was the making of a compassionate, progressive bilingual country. A modern Canada. Pearson's Canada.

THINGS DIDN'T START WELL. During the campaign, Pearson was urged to promise "One Hundred Days of Decision" from the moment his government took office; he told his advisers that this sounded like Napoleon's march to Waterloo. The Liberals settled instead on "Sixty Days of Decision," which led them to a Waterloo of their own. If giving themselves forty less days to implement an ambitious agenda was historically sound, it was politically stupid. This was one of the errors of another faltering campaign in which the Liberals blew the majority that was theirs at the outset. On April 8, they won 129 seats, the Conservatives won 95, the New Democrats won 17, and Social Credit/Creditistes won 24. Pearson quickly appointed a distinguished cabinet, including a record ten French Canadians. His big mistake was making Walter Gordon, his patrician friend and fervent nationalist, minister of finance. When Gordon brought down his budget on June 13, the fifty-third day of decision, things fell apart. The days of decision were numbered and so were those of the budget. Accelerating the process and relying on outside consultants, Gordon confidently introduced implausible nationalist measures, including a 15 percent withholding tax on dividends paid to non-residents and a 30 percent takeover tax on companies bought by foreigners. The budget was savaged by Bay Street and the markets tumbled. Gordon withdrew the taxes, in one case nineteen minutes before trading closed in eastern Canada, and offered his resignation. Pearson refused it, unwisely.

Neither Pearson nor his ministers were economic nationalists. Gordon was virtually alone in arguing, as he had in books and speeches since 1957, that Canada's economic dependence would mean the loss of its political independence. It was the raison d'être of his public life. In the 1960s, one-third of Canadian industry was foreign-owned, including half of manufacturing and 60 percent of oil and gas. As Stephen Azzi wrote in his biography of Gordon, Pearson had led his friend to believe that he shared his views (Pearson disliked confrontation and petitioners often left mistakenly thinking that he agreed with them). In fact, Pearson believed in foreign investment in developing Canada's economy. "We can maintain our economic sovereignty if we are willing to pay the price, and the price would be nationalist economic policies which would reduce our standard of living by perhaps 25 to 30 percent," he warned in 1966. "Not many Canadians are willing to do that and I don't think Canadians should have to do that." While Pearson was a nationalist, a thread that ran through his thinking from Oxford to Ottawa, he was conscious of the limits of independence in North America. "He was a status nationalist," said Jack Pickersgill in the 1970s. "He wanted the flag, the Order of Canada, ceremonial changes so Canadians could stop feeling like quasi-colonials. But he wasn't interested in economic affairs." The budget fiasco inaugurated a reign of error. Pearson disowned the budget but not its discredited author. In 1965, Gordon would advise Pearson to call an early election to win a majority. When the Liberals fell two seats short that November, Pearson accepted his resignation. In 1963, though, Pearson was more forgiving. The government acquired a reputation for ineptitude that would long over-shadow its legacy.

There would soon be bigger problems. The Front de libération du Québec was becoming the violent face of a simmering discontent in the province. A blast had killed a night watchman in an armoury in Montreal two days before Pearson took office. Less than a month later, a bomb explod-ed in a red mailbox in the tony English-speaking enclave of Westmount, maiming a sergeant. As the mood darkened that summer, the government created its promised Royal Commission on Bilingualism and Biculturalism chaired by André Laurendeau, the former influential editor of *Le Devoir* who had proposed the commission, and Davidson Dunton, a respected scholar and journalist. Two years later, the commission declared that Canada was "passing through the greatest crisis in its history." Pearson had used similar words in 1962 when he felt the first convulsions from Quebec. Canada was being shaken by a seismic change. While French-speaking Canadians were seeking political recognition, negroes were demanding equal rights in the American South. Welcome to the 1960s.

Pearson seized the moment. He would call national unity his "passionate interest" and "in some respects the most important issue of my career." National unity became a byword for addressing the demands of Quebec in particular and reassessing federal-provincial relations in general. Gordon Robertson, who was Clerk of the Privy Council in those years, recalls that Ottawa's big challenge was learning to accommodate the demands of Jean Lesage—who was not a separatist—within the federal system. The challenge was entirely new. From tax sharing to equalization, Pearson broadened the discussion to the whole country in the cheerful spirit of "co-operative federalism."

National unity wasn't just about culture and language, which Laurendeau and Dunton examined in their highly publicized travelling road show. While they consulted in 1963 and 1964, the government talked money and programs. The response to the Quiet Revolution was administrative reform: allowing Quebec to opt out of shared-cost programs while receiving compensation in cash or tax points; allowing Quebec to develop its own programs within a national framework; designing a constitutional amending formula. These were not small matters. They required intense negotiation. Unsurprisingly, Pearson revelled in domestic diplomacy. His government held a staggering 114 federal-provincial consultations in its first eighteen months, more than Diefenbaker held in six years. This was the beginning of executive federalism, which would become the battleground of Canada's Constitutional Wars, that enervating generational conflict extending from Lesage's demands for recognition in the 1960s to Lucien Bouchard's demands for independence in the 1990s. In the beginning, these conclaves bore fruit. Opting out, for example, allowed Quebec to leave some fifteen of sixty shared-cost programs in return for tax points and establishing its own programs. By 1968, Quebec's share of revenues of income tax collected in the province rose to 50 percent from 17 percent in 1963 and to 75 percent from 50 percent of succession duties. The province was demanding money to finance the expansion of the state—profitable federalism, so to speak—and Ottawa was obliging.

The crowning achievement was the Canada Pension Plan, which the Liberals had promised in 1963. Quebec objected to a uniform scheme and designed its own, which was actually better than Ottawa's. When negotiations broke down, an intergovernmental conference was called for Quebec City beginning on March 31, 1964. It broke down too, when Lesage demanded a bigger share of tax revenues. Then Lesage threatened to bring down a budget sharply increasing taxes and blaming Ottawa. The mood turned ugly. There were riots in the streets, a bomb scare at the conference, a cocktail of threats, cries, and laments. The country was in crisis again. "We went back to Ottawa thinking really that Confederation might easily break up," recalled Walter Gordon. Pearson addressed Parliament on April 14. He stressed the need for accommodation (it wasn't "capitulation or betrayal") and warned that a failure to understand "the special sensitiveness" of Quebec could destroy Canada. By way of compromise, Ottawa agreed to give the provinces more tax revenues and Quebec agreed to make its plan more like Ottawa's. It also established the right of the provinces to opt out of shared-cost programs. On April 20, a deal was announced. "Let us rejoice," enthused Claude Ryan, editor of *Le Devoir*. "I think Confederation was saved at that point," declared Stanley Knowles, the veteran New Democrat. In 1966, the Canada Pension Plan came into effect. It represented both an expansion of the welfare state and the evolution of the federal state.

Pearson played a minor role in these talks. But his speech to Parliament showed that he recognized the urgency of the problem. Judy LaMarsh, his salty minister who had been cut out of the talks, called the agreement "a sellout" and shattered Pearson's framed autographed photograph sitting on her desk. For Pearson, ever the conciliator, the Canada Pension Plan proved the country could accommodate its linguistic and regional differences.

In the same spirit, he wanted to find a new constitutional amending formula to bring about the patriation of the British North America Act of 1867. That, too, was part of his era of accommodation. But the erratic Lesage, having said that he would accept an agreed-upon formula giving Ontario and Quebec a veto over amendments, changed his mind in 1964, as his successors would as well on these delicate matters. Like every other constitutional initiative since 1927, this one died.

THE AMENDING FORMULA, opting out, bilingualism, and the Canada Pension Plan were Pearson's olive branch to Quebec. In bringing all the provinces into the process, his federal-provincial diplomacy was devoutly devolutionist. Up to then, the federal government, which had accrued great power during the Second Word War, had largely run Canada as a unitary state. It would no longer. For skeptics, and John Diefenbaker was one, there was no putting this genie back in the bottle. Pearson ignored charges of appeasement from English Canada; he thought the balance should be realigned, which is how, as John English says, Pearson "presided over the most rapid and extensive decentralization in Canadian history between 1963 and 1965." At best, this bought time for Canada and won applause in Quebec; at worst, it set in train the erosion of the federal government that would make Canada, by some measures, the most decentralized country in the world. Forty years later, as power continues to shift decisively from the centre to the regions, the Quiet Revolution has become the Quiet Devolution. In 1999, Claude Ryan said Pearson's "words on relations between Quebec and Canada are surprising even today in their openness and audacity." In Quebec, these are remembered as the halcyon days of flexible federalism.

Between 1965 and 1968, Pearson's views on Quebec hardened. Pearson's francophone ministers had become discredited by scandal, forcing out the thoughtful Maurice Lamontagne and the gifted Guy Favreau. In 1965, the Liberals recruited "the three wise men" of Quebec: Jean Marchand, Gérard Pelletier, and Pierre Trudeau. It was a *coup de grâce* that dramatically changed the conversation. Now they had Pearson's ear. Trudeau, whom Pearson made his parliamentary secretary in 1966, opposed concessions adamantly. He scoffed when Lesage made a claim on family allowances, a federal responsibility, and mused about taking control of unemployment insurance and old age pensions too, also federal programs. In coveting the whole field of social legislation, Peter C. Newman wrote, Quebec was intending "to opt out of co-operative federalism." This was special status, and from Lesage's view, it was logical. Hadn't Pearson provided the intellectual rationale for the distinctiveness of Quebec in 1963 and 1964 when he had called it "a nation within a nation" and "not a province like the others but the homeland of a people"?

That battle was never joined; in June 1966, Jean Lesage was defeated by Daniel Johnson and the Union Nationale. A more fierce nationalist, Johnson wanted "equality or independence." The rift was widening. The triumvirate from Quebec told Pearson that dealing with Quebec directly undermined the equality of the provinces and the power of MPs from Quebec. Quebec did benefit from the Canada Assistance Plan and financial support for post-secondary education. But when it came to negotiating medicare in 1966, one of the government's signal achievements, there would be no opting out; the provinces had to conform to federal standards. The same was true on vocational training. Now the nationalists in Quebec were unhappy. When Trudeau became justice minister in 1967, his profile rose and his influence grew. He dismissed Quebec's international ambitions and he urged Pearson to hang tough when Charles de Gaulle cried, "Vive le Québec libre!" in Montreal that July. Pearson did, icily telling de Gaulle that Canada did not need liberating. The chastened general cancelled his visit to Ottawa and decamped for Paris.

By 1968, Pearson was no longer the conciliator of 1963. He was more wary of Quebec. With Lesage gone, he didn't have to accommodate a friendly federalist. He had embraced the recommendations of bilingualism by Laurendeau and Dunton—indeed, without waiting for their final report, which wasn't presented until after he'd left office—he proposed a bilingual public service in 1966. In February 1968, when the federal government and the provinces met in Ottawa to discuss constitutional reform, Ottawa proposed a charter of rights, entrenched language rights, patriation, and an amending formula. There was no talk of division of powers. No talk of special status, or anything special at all. Quebec wasn't even explicitly mentioned. Now it was a province *comme tous les autres*.

To those bewitched by Pearson's early federalism, his second mandate was a disappointment. For Claude Ryan, Pearson's later years were "marked by a return to conventional thinking that was little favourable to Quebec." Recalling Pearson's soothing words about Quebec's distinctiveness, he implies that Pearson would have endorsed Quebec as "a distinct society," the heart of the ill-fated Meech Lake Accord of 1987. More pointedly, Gordon Robertson believes that had Pearson been prime minister in 1981 he "never" would have patriated the Constitution, as Trudeau did, without the consent of Quebec. Political scientist Kenneth McRoberts argues wistfully that Pearson embraced the "two-nations" theory of Confederation and his co-operative federalism, asymmetrical at its core, represented a rare opportunity for Canada.

Which was the real Pearson? There is no doubt that he heard the *cri de cœur* from Quebec. His speech in 1962 set the tone for his imaginative response to French Canada. There is also no doubt that he liked acting as a national Secretary-General, which is how he could smile through all those meetings with posturing premiers. Bilingualism is his legacy. It may be, as well, that his co-operative federalism was the only feasible response to the nationalist juggernaut at the time. Pearson was backed into a corner on the Canada Pension Plan by a more agile provincial government, and he reacted creatively. It also helped that Jean Lesage, who was a federalist, wanted a settlement. Once again, as he had at Suez, Pearson benefited from a reasonable adversary.

But this view—that Pearson embraced a distinctive Quebec, that he believed in two nations, that he saw Quebec as a homeland for French Canadians—ran its course. It is trumped by the realist who said no to Quebec on medicare, who limited opting-out, and who opposed Quebec's foreign adventures. The shift in his thinking is critical. Pearson always believed in the strengthening of the country, the whole country. Hence his emphasis on symbols and identity. True, his foremost instinct was accommodation, not confrontation, and he liked to bring people together and send them away happy. But we misinterpret his federalism as we misinterpret his internationalism. Much as he wanted domestic peace, he knew it could not come at any price; he came to realize, especially when facing Daniel Johnson, that the centre must hold. Co-operative federalism was never to be seen as a blank cheque, a country run by a *directoire* of first ministers dismantling the federal government. This was devolution by a thousand concessions. We wonder now how Pearson would have handled the separatist René Lévesque who was elected in 1976. Would there have been a peace for our conciliator to make? Could Pearson have been Pearson, then or today?

As he had waffled on isolationism in the late 1930s, Pearson waffled on nationalism in the early 1960s. Circumstances changed and he did too. His view of constitutional reform was no longer about special status, a distinct society, a division of powers, or even exclusively about

Quebec. It was Trudeau's vision of Canada and it was Trudeau, the principled federalist from Quebec, whom Pearson wanted as his successor.

FOR PEARSON, amending the Constitution, extending social welfare, and embracing official bilingualism were nation-building. So was adopting national symbols, his "status nationalism." Pearson wanted Canadians to feel like citizens rather than subjects. Canada had been detaching itself from Britain even before he entered public life in 1928. The creation of the Department of External Affairs in 1909, the Statute of Westminster in 1931, the Canadian Citizenship Act in 1947, the empowerment of the Supreme Court of Canada in 1949, the appointment of Vincent Massey as the country's first native-born Governor General in 1952—all were steps to greater autonomy. This affirmation of self culminated in 1982 with the return of the British North America Act and the entrenchment of the Charter of Rights and Freedoms. For Pearson, the most important of symbols was a national flag. The Red Ensign was Canada's flag, but it wasn't Canadian, or not as wholly Canadian as it might be; it was the banner of the British Merchant Marine with the Canadian Coat of Arms. Before Pearson, no prime minister would change it. He did.

Pearson could have announced a new flag to a partisan audience; instead, on May 17, 1964, he addressed the annual convention of the Royal Canadian Legion in Winnipeg. It was a courageous act on the part of a plucky politician. Always the reluctant soldier, he was persuaded that day to wear his seven service medals. He wanted to appeal to the veterans as one of them, enlisting their support in his crusade for "a flag that is truly distinctive and truly national in character ... a flag easily identifiable as Canada's.... Canada's own and only Canada's...." He was greeted with a chorus of boos and jeers and a phalanx of clenched fists. He continued to press his case calmly, pausing twice, bemused, when the chairman called for order. "You're selling Canada to the peasoupers!" thundered one veteran. Pearson never lost his place or his temper. He finished his remarks to restrained applause. Watching the grainy, black and white film of the prime minister in the lion's den recalls a pivotal moment in the life of a country. It wasn't so much the speech itself. Pearson was no orator. The voice is prissy, the lisp discernible. The hands are in his pockets or stabbing the air at mid-chest. The head bobs and weaves. The horn-rimmed glasses are pre–*Father Knows Best*. The power of this minor melodrama is that he is *there*, speaking his piece before a hostile crowd. He is unfazed, unruffled, Teflon before we knew the term. He is unadorned, unembellished, plain. If Pearson's leadership were architecture, the style would not be the razzle-dazzle of the Rococo. It would be Palladian—straight and formal. Listening to the veterans respond to Pearson, we understand their loyalty to the Red Ensign and their resistance to a new flag. We also understand the depth of his commitment.

Pearson presented the motion to Parliament in June. Although two of the other parties supported a new flag in principle, the Conservatives did not. John Diefenbaker, the most barnacled of the anglophiles, was apoplectic, seeming to regard a new flag as an attack on Christendom itself. Lamenting the removal of "the Christian crosses, the spiritual elements," he demanded a national plebiscite. Pearson refused. "I was determined," he recalled. "I did not care what happened. I was going to see it through and a flag was going to be endorsed by Parliament." As Trudeau would have his Constitution, Pearson would have his flag. The debate dragged on all autumn, much of it silly and hysterical. Some of Pearson's advisers wondered why the government was spending so much time and capital on this. The original design (three leaves between two blue borders on a field of white, which Diefenbaker derided as "Pearson's pennant") gave way to one of red borders and a lone red maple leaf on white.

In December, a frustrated government invoked closure, which had not been used in Parliament since the disastrous pipeline debate of 1956. The Conservatives acted as if this were the end of the world, which in a way it was—at least an end to their world, a small, colonial Canada. By the end of the 37 days of debate, there had been 308 speeches; 221 members had spoken, some more than three times. At 2:15 in the morning of December 14, the flag was passed 163 to 78. The members burst into "O Canada!" then "God Save the Queen." On February 15, 1965, the Maple Leaf was raised on the Peace Tower. Diefenbaker cried. Pearson beamed. "If our nation by God's grace endures a thousand years, this day will always be remembered as a milestone in Canada's national progress," he said. He had carried the day, and the country too. The Maple Leaf would always be Pearson's pennant. It would not extinguish nationalism—Trudeau sniffed that "Quebec doesn't give a tinker's damn about the new flag"—and it would not unify Canada as its most fervent acolytes claimed. But it was more than tinkering. Pearson was making Canada more Canadian. It was his proudest moment as prime minister.

Status nationalism didn't end there. Pearson was leading another Quiet Revolution, as historian José Igartua argues, developing and promoting a Canadian nationalism, a post-British identity. And so "Royal" began disappearing from federal institutions. The "Imperial" Privy Council vanished. As Pearson had told the Canadian Legion, the country was changing; five of eighteen million Canadians were neither English nor French. The year after the flag, he moved a motion in Parliament to make "O Canada!" the county's national anthem and "God Save the Queen" its royal anthem, which would not be adopted until 1980. Two years after the flag, he created the Order of Canada, a home-grown honours system to recognize excellence among Canadians. He hoped it would "strengthen national pride and national service," though its purpose was widely questioned after a contentious appointment in 2008. Still, thousands have received it, including Lester Pearson.

IF THINGS WERE GETTING DONE in Ottawa, it wasn't always clear to Canadians how and where. The springtime optimism of 1963—"a time to excite the daring, to test the strong and to give new promise to the timid … a time of direction and decision," as Pearson put it—had faded by summer. While Mike Pearson was no Jack Kennedy, much as he sometimes favoured his rhetoric, Canadians expected competence and decisiveness from him. That evaporated with the first budget. Soon a feckless prime minister was presiding over a new order of disorder, facing an unreconstructed opposition led by a bloviating partisan. Their *pas de deux* played out every day in a low, guttural catfight in the well of the House of Commons. It sullied rather than elevated politics; Disraeli and Gladstone they were not. Accusations flew across the floor. Criminals such as Lucien Rivard and Hal Banks became household names. The Conservatives saw high crimes when two ministers received favourable terms on furniture from a Montreal company; they ridiculed the government's "political upholstery" and demanded that it "furnish us with the facts!" Pearson, for his part, threatened the Conservatives that he would reveal the liaisons between Diefenbaker's former associate defence minister and Gerda Munsinger, a German prostitute who had also had an affair with a Russian and was considered a security risk. In 1968, journalist Patrick Nicholson called the Munsinger Affair, which exploded in March 1966, "one of the most dramatic, destructive and despicable episodes in the history of Canada's Parliament."

The scandals involved ministers from Quebec. Six were forced to resign for influence-peddling, bribery, or other sins, often more imagined than real. The most tragic was Guy Favreau, whom Pearson had seen as his successor; he resigned in 1967 and died a few months later. As with

Walter Gordon, Pearson didn't stand by Favreau and came to regret it. "A personal disaster," said Judy LaMarsh. The government was struggling. Cabinet could meet eight hours a day, two or three times a week, and decide little. The prime minister was attacked for making poor patronage appointments, many of them party hacks. From his perch in the Parliamentary Press Gallery, Peter C. Newman saw "blitzkrieg, bedlam and bad government." The image of the befuddled captain bedevilled Pearson to the end. On the evening of February 19, 1968, when he was vacationing in the Bahamas and his ministers were campaigning to succeed him, the Liberals narrowly lost a vote on a tax bill in the House. Had the Conservatives not relented, the government would have fallen and faced an early election.

Amid the Sturm und Drang, Parliament was passing a dazzling volume of legislation. Beyond official bilingualism, the Order of Canada, and the new flag, the government created the Canada Pension Plan, the Canada Assistance Plan, and the Guaranteed Income Supplement. Most important, it created medicare, which had been discussed for years. These are the keystones of the modern social security system. Tom Kent, the brainy Englishman who was responsible for much of it as Pearson's policy adviser, crowed in 1999: "The distinction of the Pearson government is clear: in no other five years was so much done to improve the circumstances of life for Canadians with average and lower incomes." It was done without deficit too; indeed, the national debt declined in those years. Pearson's government also unified the armed forces, introduced a progressive immigration act, established a federal labour code, struck a royal commission on the status of women. It created the Economic Council, the Science Council, and the Company of Young Canadians. It abolished capital punishment for a trial period of five years; conferred new rights upon consumers; liberalized laws on divorce, abortion, and homosexuality; created student loans; and supported post-secondary education. It established regulatory agencies for communications and transportation, collective bargaining for the civil service, a fund for rural development, feed grain and crop insurance. Not every program was sound and not all of them were affordable when the country went into deficit in the 1980s. But universal health care, open immigration, and institutional bilingualism would define Canada—and the self-image of its people—for the next generation and beyond.

For this, Pearson received little credit in his day. Unlike LBJ, whose legislative wizardly was also overshadowed, he wasn't fighting an unpopular war in Asia. Pearson's problem was his style, which was not self-aggrandizing or pompous. Another was his lousy salesmanship. It was why he said as he was leaving office that he hoped to be measured "by the record, not by a recording." Living in the television age, Pearson wasn't camera-ready. It wasn't just the professorial bow tie, which his handlers could change, but the manner of the man, which they couldn't. His bonhomie did not transmit well to the small screen. In a time of sit-ins and *Laugh-In*, he sounded increasingly out of touch. Born a Victorian, raised an Edwardian, he was a septuagenarian by his last year in office. As the amorous Trudeau mused about the bedrooms of the nation and spent time there, his prime minister remained prim in the parlour. In the bleached, bell-bottomed, tie-dyed 1960s, Mike looked increasingly out of place, an antiquarian in the Age of Aquarius.

ONE WOULD ASSUME that Prime Minister Pearson was busy in the world in those years. In foreign affairs, where he had more expertise than any of his predecessors, his record was thin. He did double foreign aid, send the first peacekeepers to Cyprus, and broker a compromise on Rhodesia in the Commonwealth. But by and large, Pearson left diplomacy to Paul Martin Sr., his erstwhile rival and foreign minister, even though he sometimes doubted his judgment.

The one issue that Pearson could not ignore was Canadian-American relations. Despite John Diefenbaker's whimsical promise to divert 15 percent of Canadian trade to Britain, despite Walter Gordon's strenuous efforts to reduce foreign ownership beyond his aborted budget, Canada had fallen heavily into the American orbit by the 1960s. When it came to the United States, Pearson's priority was to be a strong, dependable ally, though not an uncritical one. He was less concerned about America's economic dominance in Canada than its military adventurism in Asia. In the 1950s, it had been Korea; in the 1960s, it was Vietnam. As a member of the International Control Commission since the 1950s, Canada had been involved in Indochina and had even acted as occasional intermediary between Washington and Hanoi in 1964. Unlike Suez, which he thought morally wrong, Pearson did not condemn American objectives in Vietnam. But he became disenchanted when in March 1965 the Americans launched Operation Rolling Thunder, a sustained bombing of North Vietnam. So did many Canadians. Beyond the impact of public opinion on his minority government, Pearson worried about a wider war in Asia, perhaps with China, as well as a rift within NATO. His response—and the American reaction—produced the most dramatic and misunderstood episode of his premiership.

When Pearson was invited to address Temple University in Philadelphia on April 2, 1965, he used the occasion to propose a bombing halt. He was there to receive a humanitarian award for furthering world peace. His stature as a Nobel Laureate gave the appearance gravitas in the United States. In his remarks, Pearson said the United States had intervened to help South Vietnam, and "its motives were honourable, neither mean nor imperialistic." He said that talks had to begin with a ceasefire and a limited bombing halt could break the impasse. He suggested that the "suspension of air strikes against North Vietnam <u>at the right time</u> [underlining Pearson's] might provide Hanoi with an opportunity, if they wish to take it, to inject some flexibility into their policy without appearing to do so as the direct result of military pressure."

The next day, Pearson was invited to the presidential retreat at Camp David, Maryland. He was greeted by two ashen-faced aides and escorted to lunch, where he ate uncomfortably with Johnson and Charles Ritchie, Canada's ambassador to Washington. An aloof Johnson barked orders, took telephone calls, and ignored his guest. When Pearson asked what LBJ thought of the speech, he paused and said "awful." Then he took Pearson by the arm and led him to the terrace. For an hour, Johnson excoriated Pearson for coming to his own "backyard" and attacking his policy on Vietnam. Ritchie recalled: "He strode the terrace, he sawed the air with his arms, with upraised fist he drove home the verbal hammer blows. He talked and talked … expostulating, upbraiding, reasoning, persuading. From time to time Mike attempted a sentence—only to have it swept away on the tide." The president ripped into Pearson, claiming he had betrayed him. He said he'd been under pressure to escalate the war, even to use nuclear weapons, but he'd resisted. "Not bad for a war-monger," LBJ sniffed. His performance soon reached a climax: "Mike, only half-seated, half leaning on the terrace balustrade, was now completely silent. The President strode up to him and seized him by the lapel of his coat, at the same time raising his other arm to the heavens." Johnson warned of the consequences if the United States left Vietnam. What seemed to bother Johnson most about the speech was where Pearson had made it. "You don't come here and piss on my rug," he hissed.

Although the Americans let it be known that Johnson had dressed down Pearson that day, the hoary story of presidential dudgeon did not come to light until Ritchie told it in 1974. Pearson recalls it less graphically in his posthumous memoir in 1975. There he calls their meeting "a very good and frank talk," as if he were writing a diplomatic communiqué.

The contretemps at Camp David has become part of the Pearsonian folklore, a tale of the Earnest Canadian spanked by the Pushy American for coming to his table and speaking out of turn. Like other myths, this one has grown like kudzu. No doubt Pearson had received "the Johnson treatment," that crude, earthy, tactile manner he used to browbeat reluctant colleagues as majority leader of the U.S. Senate. To Mike, Johnson was a vulgarian, the kind of guy who could invite him to urinate with him by the side of the road on his ranch or lift his shirt for photographers to show off a surgical scar. Here, though, Johnson's tirade served to magnify Pearson's remarks, making them sound more offensive than they were. Actually, Pearson's speech in Philadelphia was mild. He made no threats and laid down no markers other than to note the support in Canada for American peacemaking in Vietnam. "We wish to be able to continue that support," he said carefully. Pearson, who had stood up to the Americans in Korea and was prepared to suffer their disapproval by recognizing Red China, was conflicted about Vietnam. He had wanted to be helpful, to say something constructive, because he worried about war with China and the use of nuclear weapons. Sound familiar? When he got home he wrote Johnson what read like a letter of apology. He applauded the bombing halt that followed on

April 7, which Johnson had been planning to do anyway. Paul Martin, who opposed the speech, said that Pearson may have actually delayed the bombing halt. While Pearson felt a need to unburden himself on Vietnam and send LBJ a message, Canada would not question the war in public again for two and a half years. Pearson had hoped that "quiet diplomacy"—the venerable practice of making objections known behind closed doors—would restrain Washington. It failed. So did public diplomacy. The war escalated sharply. What his speech did, though, was create the perception of distance between Canada and the United States on this most divisive of issues, and project a lingering image of a defiant Canada challenging the United States. This gave comfort to some Canadians.

The personal relationship between Pearson and Johnson was never warm and it never recovered. But the dressing down flattered Pearson and renewed his ebbing credential as a peacemaker, even though he wasn't one in Vietnam. While Canada did not send troops to Vietnam (as New Zealand and Australia did), it sold some $1.5 billion in weapons to the United States between 1963 and 1968. It also allowed Agent Orange, a defoliant used in Southeast Asia, to be tested in New Brunswick. Pearson saw no contradiction. Canada didn't like the war and said so in private in

Washington. But there was nothing to do beyond that. Ever the realist, Pearson knew the United States was Canada's ally and friend, that it was the guarantor of the country's prosperity and security. To break publicly might imperil that. It was much the same reasoning that had prevented him from supporting Walter Gordon.

Despite Vietnam, the relationship between the two countries flourished in the 1960s. Economic integration accelerated. While anti-Vietnam protestors marched on the American embassy in Ottawa, editorialists attacked the war, draft dodgers slipped north of the border, and agreements were signed. The most important was the Auto Pact in 1965, which secured access to the American market and assured the growth of the automobile industry in Canada for a generation. George Grant thought his former friend from London had sold out to the Americans. His response was *Lament for a Nation: The Defeat of Canadian Nationalism*, a critique of a country that had lost its soul to the Americans. While Diefenbaker and the Conservatives had stood up to Washington during the Cuban Missile Crisis and rejected nuclear weapons, he said, Pearson and the Liberals embraced them. Pearson was their "instrument," an obedient, obliging continentalist. For Grant, this was the end of an independent Canada. His view gained currency, particularly in the

1980s, when Ottawa agreed to cruise missile testing, repealed restrictions on foreign investment, dismantled the National Energy Program, and embraced free trade with the United States.

But things didn't happen as Grant thought. Canada remains an economic protectorate, to be sure, but a wealthy and sovereign one. While the nuclear weapons are long gone, Canada continues to huddle under the American nuclear umbrella, which has allowed it to spend less on national defence and finance many of Pearson's expensive social programs. In this way, the United States has subsidized a kinder society in North America. But while Canada inhales American culture, it has created a lively one of its own, particularly in arts and letters. And politically, Canada can and does resist Washington, a reality acknowledged a generation later by Mel Watkins, the eminent economist and outspoken nationalist of the 1960s. Today, he says that he isn't "so sure anymore" that economic integration has constrained Canada. "There is apparently a Canadian political culture that is alive and well in spite of—might it even be because of?—economic continentalism," he wrote in 2008. "Certainly Canada has shown more willingness to stand up to Americans imperialism than it ever did to British imperialism." It said no to the invasion of Iraq in 2003 and no to the deployment of missile defence in Canada in 2005. Grant's lament is less mournful today. Pearson knew the Americans well and understood their importance in NATO in containing communism during the Cold War. He saw Canada's prospects in North America less darkly, and he was right.

BY 1967, IT WAS TIME TO GO. Robert Stanfield had replaced John Diefenbaker. Anthony Westell of the *Toronto Star* was warning that "the Pearson cabinet is showing symptoms of disintegration that may be the prelude to collapse." Mike had promised Maryon that he would resign at seventy, which he turned on April 23. He kept his word, but not right away. It was Centennial Year. Canada was celebrating the one hundredth anniversary of Confederation and Pearson wanted to host the party. This was the sweetest of times for Canada, so brimming with optimism that three decades later the incomparable Pierre Berton called his chronicle of the centenary *The Last Good Year*. Beyond Charles de Gaulle's gaucherie, nothing could spoil the reverie. For all the toil and trouble of its politics, Canadians were giddy in 1967. In communities everywhere, there were centennial projects—libraries, parks, arenas. The big celebration was Expo 67, the glittering futuristic world's fair in Montreal, which drew fifty million visitors.

On December 14, without warning, Pearson announced his resignation. He had spoken to no one but Maryon. Less than four months later the Liberals chose Pierre Trudeau, who returned to Parliament and dissolved it so quickly that he deprived Pearson of the customary tributes accorded a retiring prime minister by his colleagues. It was another opportunity lost to cast his legacy. In his diary, Pearson scrawled: "tough." On April 20, 1968, Pearson went to Rideau Hall for the last time as prime minister. It had been fifty years since he had left the military, forty years since he had entered the government, twenty years since he had entered politics, ten years since he had become leader, five years since he had become prime minister. It had been a long, wonderful ride. When he emerged after handing his resignation to the Governor General, Roland Michener, his old teammate from Oxford, he shrugged and told a gaggle of reporters: "Call me Mike, now."

MIKE AND MARYON went on holiday to Ireland and returned to their "rose-covered cottage" in Rockcliffe. Pearson had no talent for tending roses and no time either. In the few years he had left, there would be a deluge of offers and accolades. Pearson was given the Order of Merit by the Queen at Buckingham Palace, a rare honour. He was named chancellor of Carleton University, where he led a popular seminar on international affairs. He chaired the Commission on International Development, a blue-ribbon panel created by the World Bank, which boldly proposed that developed nations contribute 1 percent of their wealth to the developing world, establishing the international standard that Canada has never met almost forty years later. He was the first chairman of the International Development Research Centre and honorary chairman of the Montreal Expos and the Ottawa Rough Riders. He gave lectures and interviews, travelled widely (seventy-five thousand miles for the commission alone), collected honorary degrees. Most important, he began his memoirs. When Escott Reid warned him that his many obligations would get in the way of writing, he agreed and accepted more.

The first volume was published in October 1972. It was droll, modest, warm, characteristically self-deprecating, and selectively revealing. That autumn the cancer that had taken Pearson's right eye in 1970 returned. Time was short; he was running out of lives. He set to work furiously on the rest of the memoirs, drafting sections of the second and third volumes. He was dying. When Keith Davey went to see him late that autumn, they talked about the dismal fortunes of the Maple Leafs. "It's a crisis you're going to have to face alone," said Mike. Around Christmas, he fell into a coma. John Diefenbaker asked Canadians to pray for him. Even an appeal from his old adversary was not enough. In the late evening of December 27, 1972, at seventy-five years old, Lester Bowles Pearson died.

CHAPTER NINE

The Middle Distance

On the wall of the Pearson Study at Laurier House is a cartoon drawn by Duncan Macpherson of the *Toronto Star* in April 1964, when Canada was in a crisis of unity. It presents the prime minister as baseball player in four frames. In the first, he cringes as a ball bounces off his head. In the second, he chases the ball, glove extended. In the third, he is on his back in a cloud of dust, legs akimbo. In the fourth, he emerges smiling and triumphant—glasses dangling, cap off, hair askew—ball in glove. The caption reads: "The Old Smoothie." In power, Lester Pearson often looked old but rarely smooth. From the budget imbroglio of June 1963 to the parliamentary defeat of February 1968, he lurched from crisis to crisis. Some wondered if he actually *preferred* hanging from a precipice. If it wasn't a question of impropriety or ineptitude in his government, it was indecision and inconstancy. No wonder Canadians denied Pearson a majority in 1965. No wonder almost half wanted him to retire in 1967.

No wonder more than two-thirds could not name a single accomplishment of his government in 1968.

Lo and behold, amid the confusion, Lester Pearson was getting things done. His was the one of the most productive governments in Canadian history, even if his law-making was as messy as stuffing sausages at Armour and Company. In the baseball cartoon, Pearson's favourite, Macpherson is playing on the impasse between Ottawa and Quebec over a national pension scheme. He labels Mike's glove "Canada Pension Plan" and the ball "Canadian Unity." Pearson shambles, shuffles, and stumbles, Macpherson wants us to know, but he catches the ball. *He always catches the ball.*

And so it was on medicare and student loans and any one of the panoply of programs established in the go-go years of the 1960s. The Liberals were completing the country's social safety net. Pearson's agenda followed Mackenzie King's as Lyndon Johnson's Great Society followed Franklin Roosevelt's New Deal. The time was right. The economy was surging (month after month of unprecedented expansion) and the country was leaning left (the Liberals and New Democrats even had exploratory talks on merging in 1965). Pearson's leadership was always more about direction than detail. He knew what he wanted to do even if he went about it in a long, hard, circuitous way. They hadn't called him Herr Zigzag for nothing.

Unlike Trudeau's Just Society, Pearson's Canada never had a name. Historically, it has suffered a kind of identity theft. Because it was born in crisis, because it emerged incrementally over five years, because it was not boxed, wrapped, and tied with a red ribbon, the impact of his leadership has emerged only very slowly. It has taken time for us to see Pearson for what he is: a transformational figure between the old and new Canada. Only recently has his legacy caught up with him. In a way it recalls Churchill's description of Nazi-occupied Poland as "a rock, which may for a time be submerged by a tidal wave, but which remains a rock." Hidden though it was by the smoke of scandal and turmoil, Pearson's record remains a record. It speaks to us because it is us.

Time offers a yardstick as well as a paintbrush. After the steely Pierre Trudeau, the hyperbolic Brian Mulroney, the cautious Jean Chrétien, the fumbling Paul Martin Jr., and the dour Stephen Harper, we appreciate the character of Lester Pearson. We miss his generosity, humour, and candour. After the upheaval of four decades—inflation and unemployment, debt and deficit, nationalism in Quebec and alienation in the West, the expansion and contraction of the state, the rise of the provinces—we appreciate his stewardship. In the context of today's minority government, and the general decline of civility in politics, the 1960s don't look so shrill or chaotic or antagonistic. And Pearson's record certainly doesn't look so thin.

When Chou En-lai was famously asked what he thought of the impact of the French Revolution two centuries later, he said it was too early to say. Arthur Koestler, the author, suggested it takes fifty years to assess a revolution. We see the 1960s more clearly now than then. In 2003, a survey of historians and thinkers overwhelmingly chose Pearson as the most effective prime minister since 1945. Like us, they wisely remember his achievements more than his demons. Lucien Rivard? Hal Banks? Who cares? Peter C. Newman, who saw it all, once told Diefenbaker: "You are a great man, sir." More likely, Diefenbaker was a great story. Pearson was a great man.

He was great before he became prime minister. He was the ablest foreign minister of his day. For revisionists, we know, he and his Canada were overstated; these contrarians in search of a corrective to his lustre mine the public record and find, deep down, a vein of low-grade ore that convinces them Pearson's reputation was made of fool's gold. Yet they fail to give him due credit for showing up, for simply being there, in the world, with imagination and moxie, where no

Canadian had been before. It wasn't by accident that so many, so often, asked Pearson to lead in international councils. He knew how.

His stature rests on more than Suez or peacekeeping. It is the weight of almost three decades of statecraft, in forums big and small, seeing the big questions. In his time, he championed international organization and collective security without anxiety about the loss of national sovereignty, far ahead of his time. While it is true that Canada did not always wield the influence it sought at the United Nations, Pearson never walked away. He knew that it was our best hope. It still is. Having moved Canada away from an ebbing Britain, he hoped that the United Nations would become a counterweight to the surging United States. He tried to lessen the chances of thermonuclear war, as he called it, and he wanted a redistribution of the world's wealth, his last hurrah for the World Bank, to improve the human condition.

Michael Bliss, the respected historian, called Pearson a good man for the middle innings. It's an astute assessment. Pearson knew his limits. Had he been a runner rather than a pitcher, he would have been a good man for the middle distance. Not for him the sprints, though on days he had speed enough. Not for him the marathon, though on days he had stamina enough. The middle distance. He was most comfortable there. He was neither overreaching nor underachieving. Steady rather than flashy, pragmatic rather than ideological. He would not govern as long as his successor or predecessor—in fact, his five years were less than Diefenbaker's, Bennett's, Borden's, and many others—but he would do more. He would make no promise of a just society, just a better one, which his no-name government came closer to achieving. He knew he could solve Suez but not Hungary. He knew you could only go so far with the Americans—or against them. He talked less of perfection than improvement. Muddling through was his method. His name was Mike, not Michael, and he never thought that he was the guy for the long run and he never expected to go on and on. Which is why he quit when he did, as Bliss notes, and left his office to the man he did.

Failures? Of course. His Canada was too silent at the League of Nations and too ignored in the Second World War. He wanted a greater commitment from the United Nations to a permanent peacekeeping force. He wished to make NATO more a political community than a military alliance. He wasn't able to use diplomacy, quiet or loud, to restrain Lyndon Johnson in his quagmire in Vietnam.

Yet what is most telling about Pearson's diplomacy is that it has been adopted or imitated, in one form or another, by

every prime minister since. Trudeau pursues his international peace mission as his swansong. Mulroney joins the
Organization of American States. Chrétien promotes the
International Criminal Court and a global ban on land-
mines. Martin proposes the G20. Harper champions NATO
in Afghanistan. In 2008, the *Globe and Mail* says Stéphane
Dion's stand on Afghanistan means that he could not be "the
peace candidate in anglophone Canada, thereby denying
himself the mantle of Lester Pearson." In foreign policy, all
successors, real or aspiring, labour in Pearson's shadow. Then
again, to be Pearsonian is to be Canadian.

Oh, you could see him today, bright and bouncy, at the
podium of the General Assembly. Pleading for a humanitarian response to Darfur. Trying to forestall the invasion of Iraq.
Lobbying for the Responsibility to Protect. Warning about
global warming. Worrying about North Korea and Iran. Or,
at home, lamenting our failing internationalism, particularly
the decline of his beloved department. Sixty years after he
became minister of external affairs, he would be heartsick to
see his chair filled by some of the pygmies and poseurs who
have followed him. How has it come to this?

Contradictions? Of course. Yet Pearson isn't impossible to
paint, as Peter C. Newman says. Nor was he the paradox that
historians suggest. As there was order in the disorder, there

was consistency in the inconsistency. The consistency was Canada. The unbroken theme of his life is Canada, an idea of Canada as an autonomous nation, casting off imperial shackles and seizing responsibility, building itself at home and projecting itself abroad. A Canada of self-confidence rather than self-effacement. No modern prime minister gave more of himself to his country. Pearson spent more than half his life—some forty-three of his seventy-five years—as soldier, diplomat, and politician in the service of Canada.

Intellectually, as John English tells us, he ranged far from his roots and transcended them. Temperamentally, though, he remained of the manse. The reserve and modesty he learned there were thoroughly Canadian. So were the self-deprecating humour, the quiet idealism, and the common sense that made him so agreeable. While Canadians denied Pearson big mandates, they never disliked him. Many revered and respected him; in fact, old associates still refer to him today as "Mr. Pearson." In 2004, Canadians voted him one of the ten greatest Canadians. A country disinclined to remember its leaders remembers him better than most, affixing his name to athletic trophies and to a school of peacekeeping. Not bad for a dead white male, Irish and Christian, unilingual and anglophile, raised a century ago in the parsonages and playing fields of rock-ribbed Ontario. Not bad for a diplomat in striped pants, without dash, verve, or sex appeal. Or a lisping, rumpled politician without wealth or showmanship. Not bad for a guy named Mike who retired to his basement.

Today, more than ever, we recognize in him three national traits: moderation, that willingness to seek compromise that has served Canada well from the Quebec Act to the Constitution Act; pragmatism, that sense of the possible that ensures a country this big and diverse survives; and ambiguity, that instinct to blur differences rather than define them.

Pearson particularly liked this aphorism: "It is not within our power to command success. But we can do more. We can deserve it." How he did! As a soldier, he went to war and saved lives, including his own. As a sportsman, he won even when he lost. As a statesman, he made Canada's interests at one with the larger world. As a politician, he resurrected his party. As prime minister, he made his country at once gentler and bolder, saw the rising threat of sectionalism, and preserved Canada for another day.

In the end, though, we remember most his humanity. It was Pearson who took his dying friend, Hume Wrong, to the hospital in 1954 and stayed at his side until he expired thirty-six hours later. And who wrote to Landon Pearson, his daughter-in-law abroad (as her family hadn't), that her father was dying and she ought to come home now. And, in retirement, refused an invitation to the White House to visit Richard Nixon, whom he loathed. Pearson knew himself. He could say, without artifice, that he served in the military "without any distinction whatsoever, but as cheerfully as possible." If he didn't excel in the art of politics, this was because he was not mean enough. But he was tougher than we knew. He had many lives, more than a cat, and he earned success in all of them.

WHEN IT WAS OVER, his body lay in an oak coffin, draped with the Maple Leaf, in the Parliament of Canada. The Royal Canadian Legion, whose members had once jeered him, sent a spray of poppies. Twelve thousand people filed past. He had a state funeral, at which mourners from around the world sang hymns and read psalms. On December 31, under gunmetal skies and a veil of rain, they carried him to a pioneer cemetery above the Village of Wakefield, in the Gatineau Hills, where he had rambled with Norman Robertson and Hume Wrong and imagined a better world. There he was buried beside them. He would be joined by Maryon in 1989 and Geoffrey in 2008.

Today, the Maple Leaf flutters from a tall flagpole. The cemetery lies near the top of a hill, falling softly to a thick stand of trees. They say, years ago, when those trees were shorter, you could see the Peace Tower. They say, on a quiet day, you could hear the murmur of its bells. Neither is so today. From where he rests, though, the skies are always sunny and the view is always fair, especially the gentle meadow in the middle distance.

1897	Lester Bowles Pearson is born April 23 in Newtonbrook, Ontario.
1913	Pearson enrols at Victoria College, University of Toronto.
1915	He enlists as a private in the Canadian Army Medical Corps.
1916	He serves in the Balkans as a stretcher-bearer.
1917	He joins the Royal Flying Corps as a pilot in England and is injured in a road accident in London.
1918	Pearson is invalided home. He suffers a nervous breakdown and is discharged from the army.
1919	He returns for a last term at the University of Toronto and graduates in June.
1919	He takes a job as a sausage-stuffer at a subsidiary of Armour and Company in Hamilton, Ontario.

1920	He works as a clerk with Armour and Company in Chicago.
1921	Pearson returns to Canada and sails for Oxford University, St. John's College.
1923	He begins teaching in the Department of History, University of Toronto.
1925	Pearson marries Maryon Elspeth Moody in Winnipeg August 22.
1927	His son, Geoffrey Arthur Holland Pearson, is born.
1928	Pearson enters the Department of External Affairs as first secretary.
1929	His daughter, Patricia Lillian Pearson, is born.
1930	He attends the London Naval Conference.
1931	Pearson serves as the secretary to the Royal Commission on Grain Futures.
1934	He becomes the secretary to the Royal Commission on Price Spreads and Mass Buying.
1934	He is awarded an Order of the British Empire (OBE) for his work on the royal commission.

1935   Pearson is appointed to the Canadian High Commission in London as political secretary.

1939   Pearson takes home leave. Anticipating the war, he returns to London days before the war breaks out.

1941   He is appointed assistant undersecretary, Ottawa.

1942   He is appointed minister-counsellor to the Canadian legation in Washington, D.C.

1943   He serves as chairman of the FAO Interim Commission.

1944   He is appointed envoy extraordinary and minister plenipotentiary in Washington, D.C.

1945   Pearson is appointed ambassador to the United States.

1946   He is appointed undersecretary of state for external affairs.

1948   He is appointed secretary of state for external affairs September 10 and is elected as the Member of Parliament for Algoma East October 25. Pearson is re-elected seven times.

1949   The North Atlantic Treaty Organization
        (NATO) is established.

1950   Pearson attends the Colombo Conference
        in Colombo, Ceylon.

1951–52 He serves as chairman of the NATO Council.

1952   He is elected president of Seventh Session,
        UN General Assembly.

1956   Pearson is one of the "three wise men" to
        examine NATO.

1956   He introduces the critical peacekeeping
        resolution to end the Suez Crisis.

1957   The Liberals are defeated. Pearson wins
        the Nobel Peace Prize.

1958   He is elected leader of the Liberal Party of
        Canada and leads the party to the worst
        defeat in its history March 31.

1960   The Kingston Conference begins the renewal
        of the Liberal Party.

1962   Pearson proposes a bilingualism commission.
        The Liberals win ninety-nine seats in the
        election.

1963   He reverses the party stand on nuclear war-
        heads. He is elected April 8 with a minority
        government and assumes office April 23.

1964   The Canada Pension Plan is negotiated.

1965   The Maple Leaf flag is adopted. The Liberals
        are re-elected with a minority government.

1966   Medicare comes into effect.

1967   Pearson announces his resignation in
        Centennial Year.

1968   Pearson retires in April.

1969   He serves as chairman of a seminal study
        of international developmental assistance.

1972   Pearson dies December 27 and is buried
        December 31, in Wakefield, Quebec.

Unlike most prime ministers of Canada, there is a fair amount written on Lester Pearson. We are also fortunate to have what he himself has written, both his comprehensive memoir and his collections of articles, lectures, and speeches. Together they illuminate the man and his times.

We begin with *Mike: The Memoirs of the Rt. Hon. Lester B. Pearson* (Toronto: University of Toronto Press, 1972). He published the first of three volumes in the fall of 1972, shortly before he died in December. It is very much *him*. Knowing his end was near, he rushed to draft sections of the second and third volumes, which were completed by editors drawing on Pearson's letters, diaries, and speeches. The remaining volumes were published posthumously in 1973 and 1975 but lack the authenticity of the first. In retirement, Pearson also published *Words and Occasions* (Toronto: University of Toronto Press, 1970), an invaluable anthology of writing on subjects ranging from sports to politics drawn from all periods of his busy life. Another useful collection is *The Four Faces of Peace* (Toronto: McClelland and Stewart, 1964).

The indispensable biography of Lester Pearson is *Shadow of Heaven: The Life of Lester Pearson 1897–1948* (Toronto: Lester Orpen and Dennys, 1989) and *The Worldly Years: The Life of Lester Pearson 1949–1972* (Toronto: Alfred A. Knopf Canada, 1992) by John English, a professor of history and a former Liberal Member of Parliament. Exhaustive in scale, lyrical in tone, no other work on the man has its authority. Though less ambitious, John Beal (*The Pearson Phenomenon* [Toronto: Longman's Canada, 1964]) and Bruce Thordarson (*Lester Pearson: Diplomat and Politician* [Toronto: University of Oxford Press, 1974]) have contributed sprightly biographies written in the decade before and after his death.

The other essential work is *The Distemper of Our Times* (Toronto: McClelland and Stewart, 1968) by Peter C. Newman, an account of Pearson as prime minister published the year he left office. Newman was the foremost journalist of his generation. His reportage and analysis are sharp, colourful, and critical. Newman revisits Pearson (borrowing winning phrases and ideas from *Distemper*) in *Here Be Dragons: Telling Tales of People, Passion and Power* (Toronto: McClelland and Stewart, 2004), his splendid autobiography. Newman and English divide the world of Pearson between them, and Canada owes both a debt of gratitude.

Another priceless source on the man and his period are the pair of oral histories compiled by Peter Stursberg (*Lester Pearson and the Dream of Unity* [Toronto: Doubleday Canada, 1978] and *Lester Pearson and the American Dilemma* [Toronto: Doubleday Canada, 1980]). Stursberg, another great journalist, interviewed Pearson's friends, colleagues, and associates in the 1970s and published their edited recollections. He has deposited the full transcripts in the National Library. They are a gold mine for historians, whatever the dangers of oral history. Less good as a contemporary account but still useful is Patrick Nicholson's *Vision and Indecision* (Toronto: Longman's Canada, 1968).

To understand the civil service in which Pearson served, see *The Ottawa Men: The Civil Service Mandarins 1935–1957* (Toronto: Oxford University Press, 1982), the finest of historian J.L. Granatstein's many fine books. Here, as well, the elegant recollections of Escott Reid (*Radical Mandarin: The Memoirs of Escott Reid* [Toronto: University of Toronto Press, 1989] are important. So are the incomparable diaries of Charles Ritchie: *The Siren Years: A Canadian Diplomat Abroad* (Toronto: Macmillan of Canada, 1974); *Diplomatic Passport: More Undiplomatic Diaries, 1946–1962* (Toronto: Macmillan of Canada, 1981); and *Storm Signals: More Undiplomatic Diaries, 1962–1971* (Toronto: Macmillan of Canada, 1983). For a flavour of the man in his time, see *Maclean's, Saturday Night*, and the major Canadian newspapers, as well as *The New York Times* and *The Observer*. As foreign minister, in particular, Pearson was prominently and favourably featured in all of them.

The Public Archives of Canada also has Pearson's diaries and letters, as well as clippings, speeches, and memoranda. Some are open to the public, some not. In this book, I have quoted from the newly deposited letters between Pearson and his friend Margaret Ryan, when he was Leader of the Opposition.

Also helpful are *Seize the Day: Lester Pearson and Crisis Diplomacy* (Ottawa: Carleton University Press, 1993), Geoffrey Pearson's eloquent analysis of Pearsonian Diplomacy, as well as *Anecdotage*, his slender memoir printed privately in 2007, a year before he died. On Maryon Pearson, see chapters in Heather Robertson's trenchant *More Than a Rose: Prime Ministers, Wives and Other Women* (Toronto: Seal Books, 1991) and Susan Riley's *Political Wives: Wifestyles of the Rich and Famous* (Toronto: McClelland and Stewart, 1989).

Our understanding of Pearson has been enriched by many useful contributions in the last quarter-century. For a larger view of some of the people and the issues of Pearson's time, see Christina McCall Newman's *Grits: An Intimate Portrait of the Liberal Party* (Toronto: Macmillan of Canada, 1982); Stephen Azzi's *Walter Gordon: The Rise of Canadian Nationalism* (Montreal: McGill-Queens University Press, 1999); Graham Fraser's thorough study of the history of bilingualism in Canada, *Sorry I Don't Speak French: Confronting the Canadian Crisis That Won't Go Away* (Toronto: McClelland and Stewart, 2006); and William Christian's revealing *George Grant: A Biography* (Toronto: University of Toronto Press, 1993).

Among Pearson's contemporaries, see Bruce Hutchison's poignant essay "The Lonely Extrovert" in *Mr. Prime Minister 1867–1964* (Toronto: Longman's Canada, 1964, 1967). Tom Kent and James Coutts, who advised Pearson, have written admiring tributes to his government in *Policy Options*, the monthly periodical of the Institute for Research on Public Policy in Montreal. Other essays on Pearson of varying quality from former diplomats and scholars have appeared in the years since his death in *International Journal*, the journal of the Canadian Institute of International Affairs.

Historian Norman Hillmer has edited a superb volume of essays on Pearson (*Pearson: The Unlikely Gladiator* [Montreal:

McGill Queen's University Press, 1999]). It offers original views on his life and contributions from Pearson's contemporaries such as Gordon Robertson and Claude Ryan. Michael Bliss pens a provocative assessment of Pearson in *Some Honourable Men: The Descent of Canadian Politics from Macdonald to Chrétien* (Toronto: HarperCollins, 1994, 2004). Historian C.P. Champion presents his unorthodox view in a spirited essay on Lester Pearson and the flag ("A Very British Coup," *Journal of Canadian Studies* 40: 3, Fall 2006) as well as "Mike Pearson at Oxford: War, Varsity, and Canadianism" (*Canadian Historical Review* 88: 2, June 2007). Another revisionist view of Pearson comes from historian Adam Chapnick in *The Middle Power Project: Canada and the Founding of the United Nations* (Vancouver: University of British Columbia Press, 2005). Greg Donaghy, a leading historian at Foreign Affairs and International Trade Canada, presents a persuasive study of relations with the United States in the Pearson years in *Tolerant Allies: Canada & the United States 1963–1968* (Montreal: McGill-Queen's University Press, 2002).

Finally, I have drawn on my earlier work on Lester Pearson in *While Canada Slept: How We Lost Our Place in the World* (Toronto, McClelland and Stewart, 2003) and "Canada, the United States, and Vietnam, 1963–1968: Lester Pearson and the Failure of Quiet Diplomacy," my unpublished master's thesis, which was completed in 1983 at the Norman Paterson School of International Affairs at Carleton University in Ottawa.

ACKNOWLEDGMENTS

When John Ralston Saul approached me to write a biography of Lester Pearson for this ambitious historical series he is editing for Penguin Canada, I was delighted to say yes. I have been intrigued by Pearson since I was a graduate student in international affairs, when I wrote my thesis on the failure of Quiet Diplomacy during the Vietnam War. Years later, I returned to Pearson in exploring the decline of Canada's internationalism in *While Canada Slept: How We Lost Our Place in the World.* To this volume of Extraordinary Canadians, John gently made sound suggestions on theme and structure, as well as offering an imaginative interpretation of Pearson's place in modern Canada. John Ralston Saul is an extraordinary Canadian himself.

I owe great thanks to Heather Sangster and the Strong Finish team, who edited the manuscript carefully, simplified unwieldy prose, and cheerfully shepherded the book through the production process. Graham Fraser, Canada's commissioner of official languages and a former journalist, shared his thoughts with me on the origins of official bilingualism. Colin Robertson, a diplomat and a devoted Pearsonian, kindly read the manuscript. Peter C. Newman, the author and journalist, happily answered my queries on the politics of the 1960s. Boo Leslie, the daughter of Brooke Claxton, graciously shared her memories of growing up in Pearson's Rockcliffe.

Geoffrey Pearson talked to me about his father, as he had often over the years. When I saw him last February, he was funny, tart, and unusually sentimental. He died unexpectedly shortly after our conversation. No son could have been more devoted to the memory and ideals of his father. This book is dedicated to him.

Landon Pearson reflected on the character of her father-in-law and his marriage to Maryon. She was generous, frank, and expansive in what was a difficult time for her, for which I am intensely grateful.

Having spent the last year in Berlin, I could not have written this biography without my superb research assistant, Kristina Roic, a writer and editor in Ottawa. This is our second collaboration on a book, and Kristina remains unfailingly thorough, reliable, and conscientious. She found out-of-print books, unearthed old magazine and newspaper articles, organized my visits to the National Archives, and shipped material across the Atlantic. She also reviewed the manuscript. Once again, she has been indispensable.

My deepest gratitude goes to my wife, Mary Gooderham, an author, journalist, and editor. There is no longer anything I write that Mary does not read before I submit it, demanding a standard of clarity and economy of writing that I seldom reach. Without her indulgence and love, this biography of Lester Pearson would not have come to be.

Andrew Cohen
June 27, 2008
Berlin